D1484119

FRANK
SINATRA
OL' BLUE EYES

FRANK SINATRA
OL' BLUE EYES

BY NORM GOLDSTEIN THE ASSOCIATED PRESS

Holt, Rinehart and Winston
NEW YORK

Copyright © 1982 by The Associated Press

All rights reserved, including the right to reproduce this
book or portions thereof in any form.

Published by Holt, Rinehart and Winston,
383 Madison Avenue, New York, New York 10017.

Published simultaneously in Canada by Holt, Rinehart and
Winston of Canada, Limited.

Library of Congress Cataloging in Publication Data

Goldstein, Norm.
  Frank Sinatra.

  Discography: p.
  Filmography: p.
  1. Sinatra, Frank, 1915–   . 2. Singers—United
States—Biography. I. Title.
ML420.S565G6 1982   784.5′0092′4 [B]   82-11939
ISBN 0-03-061919-X
ISBN 0-03-061921-1 (pbk.)

First Edition

Designer: J. Paul Kirouac, A Good Thing, Inc.
Printed in the United States of America

10 9 8 7 6 5 4 3 2 1

The Associated Press thanks the following producers
and distributors of the films of Frank Sinatra: Columbia
Pictures, Embassy Pictures, Metro-Goldwyn-Mayer,
Paramount Pictures, RKO Pictures, 20th Century-Fox,
United Artists, Universal-International, Warner Bros.;
A-C Productions, A.M.B.L. Productions, Arcola-Millfield,
Artanis Productions, Arwin Productions, Canterbury
Productions, Carlyle Productions, Dorchester
Productions, Essex-Claude Productions, Essex-George
Sidney Productions, Essex-Tandem Productions, Frank
Roth-Eaton Productions, Samuel Goldwyn Productions,
G.S.-Posa Films International, Greene-Rouse
Productions, Joel Productions, Kent Productions, Libra
Productions, Melnor Films, M.C. Productions, Mirisch-
Llenroc-Batjac, P-C Productions, P-R Productions, Sam
Co., Sinatra Enterprises-Seven Arts Productions,
Sincap Productions, Stanley Kramer Productions,
Suffolk-Cummings Productions, Michael Todd
Productions.
    Special photo acknowledgement to The Miami Herald
and The Trenton Times.

ISBN 0-03-061919-X HARDBOUND
ISBN 0-03-061921-1 PAPERBACK

Sinatra rehearsing for "Hit Parade" in 1944.

It was the end of 1942, neither the best nor the brightest of years for the United States, which had been officially at war since the previous December. The war masked the traditionally gay New Year celebrations with a weird quality, melancholy replacing merriment in Times Square, that ground zero of the annual observance.

All daily living revolved around the war, from front page news about the battlefront—Soviet allies had surrounded 22 enemy divisions around Stalingrad; British and German ships were battling in northern waters—to letters from the sons, husbands, and fathers who wrote so optimistically from over there.

Life at home went on as well as it could under the circumstances. The big bands were still the great popular entertainment lures of the day, from the live stage to that relatively new electronic medium, the radio. *Down Beat* magazine's annual poll named Duke Ellington the Number One swing band of the year, Benny Goodman was second, and Tommy Dorsey and his orchestra won the "sweet band" division. Helen O'Connell announced she was leaving Jimmy Dorsey's band; she was to be replaced by Kitty Kallen.

"Star Spangled Rhythm," an all-star variety movie with 43 "names"—count 'em, 43—opened at the Paramount Theater, that grand old house at Broadway and 44th Street. On stage—live—the ads proclaimed: "In Person: Benny Goodman and His Famous Orchestra." Appearing with the band were a young singer named Peggy Lee, a trio of impersonators known as the Radio Rogues, and a couple of Harlem dancer-comedians billed as Moke & Poke.

"Doors Open 8 a.m.," read one sign, "Buy War Bonds," another. There was even an "Extra Added Attraction."

The movie, which listed Bing Crosby, Victor Moore, Betty Hutton, and Bob Hope among its credited stars, was a "whopping big benefit show."

The audience was made up mostly of young girls, unescorted because of the war. They wore the short, just-above-the-ankle socks that gave rise to the term "bobbysoxer." These girls had come primarily to hear the "Extra Added Attraction."

The bandleader introduced his new singer rather matter of factly: "And now, Frank Sinatra."

A skinny young fellow, a "wet mop" of an entertainer barely visible on either side of the microphone he clutched so tightly—seemingly for support—stepped cautiously through the scrim. He was greeted with shrieks and moans, which quite shocked the better-known bandleader and his musicians.

The young singer began with a love song, crooned in a pleasantly rich, highly stylized baritone voice. It sent his audience—mostly those bobbysoxers—into swoons. They adored, they worshipped, they screeched.

And Francis Albert Sinatra, then 27 years old but looking much younger, skyrocketed to a position of fame which, in a career spanning nearly 50 years, he has never had to relinquish.

For almost half a century, Frank Sinatra has beguiled us with a million memorable melodies and established an indelible reputation, not only as a singing sensation, but also as a movie star and a public figure of such prominence that events in his personal as well as his professional life are always "news."

"The Voice," "Chairman of the Board," "The Bony Baritone," "Sultan of Swoon," "Ol' Blue Eyes," "Mr. Show Business"—these are some of the affectionate epithets that have been showered on Frank Sinatra over the years. Loved and feared, gifted and paradoxical, charming and intolerant, generous and hated, impetuous and admired, he is an entertainment giant of enormous talent, however unpredictable his behavior and temperament.

Indeed, Sinatra defies classification. Probably no words on a page can describe him. After all is said, written, debated, and questioned about him, he remains simply—or maybe not so simply—Frank Sinatra: a phenomenon.

And he did it his way.

The "way" began in Catania, an ancient industrial seaport city on Sicily, an island seemingly kicked off the toe of Italy. On the east coast of the island, Catania sits on the plains of Mount Etna, made fertile by the lava belching from that still-active volcano. The ancient city had been conquered by man, or destroyed by nature, at least seven times in its history; each time it was rebuilt.

Volcanic, sturdy, resilient: it seems that all of Frank Sinatra's most enduring qualities are symbolized by that island in the Mediterranean.

It was from that background that Anthony Martin Sinatra came to settle in Hoboken, New Jersey, the industrial seaport across the Hudson River from New York City that served as host and haven to immigrants of so many nationalities: Italians; Jews; Irish. It was in Hoboken that he met and married Natalie Garaventi—always known as Dolly—daughter of a lithographer's stonegrinder from Genoa.

Dolly, a strawberry blonde who was much more outgoing than her husband, became prominent in local Democratic politics, and eventually a ward leader. She used her influence to get Marty Sinatra a job as a city fireman. A ruddy, tattooed bantamweight, Marty Sinatra had been a boxer—under the name Marty O'Brien, since Irish names were more popular in the ring at the time—then worked briefly as a boilermaker. For a while he ran a tavern, bought with money borrowed from Dolly's mother. He worked his way up to

the rank of captain in the fire department and stayed on the job for 24 years, until his retirement.

At home, however, Dolly was the captain; she ruled the household.

On December 12, 1915, in their two-family house at 415 Monroe Street, Dolly and Marty Sinatra welcomed their first and only child. They named him Francis Albert. The baby almost didn't make it.

He was a huge baby and Dr. Peterson had trouble with the delivery. In an effort to extricate the 13½-pound infant, he accidentally ripped the head with the forceps and tore away one earlobe, leaving scars on the left cheek. "We'll have to try and save the mother," announced the doctor that chilly Sunday morning.

But the baby's grandmother wouldn't accept that the boy was stillborn. Rosa Garaventi ran an Italian grocery, but she knew something about midwifery. After all, she had nine children. She snatched up the new-born baby and put him under a cold water faucet. He drew his first breaths, and lived.

When he was six months old, young Francis Albert Sinatra was sent to live,

Following a performance October 22, 1978 at New York's Radio City Music Hall, Frank is honored by the Hoboken, New Jersey, Fire Department. These men all served with Sinatra's father, Martin Sinatra, when he was a captain with the Department.

temporarily, with his grandmother; he also spent a great deal of time with a neighbor, Mrs. Goldberg.

Hoboken in those days was a tough waterfront town. And young Frank quickly learned how to survive in it. Despite his scrawny appearance, he was a scrapper even as a kid and wouldn't shy away from a fight.

"You can't realize now what life was like in those days," he later said, speaking of his boyhood in the Depression years. "In my neighborhood, you literally had to fight for survival. Italians, Irish, Jews, Negroes, and heaven help an Italian kid who wandered into the Irish part of town.

"I had my first big fight when I was nine. I can remember rolling on the floor in a pool hall. I had plenty of fights after that."

At 15, he dropped out of Demarest High School in Hoboken. Dolly insisted he stay in school until he was 16, so he went to the Drake Business School for a few months. He got an 11-dollar-a-week job delivering papers for the *Jersey Observer,* which was later taken over by the *Jersey Journal.* He worked, too, as a copy boy, getting coffee for the "desk" and the reporters and running errands. Later, he showed an interest in sports and was allowed to do some sports writing.

John Hopkins, of the *Journal* copy desk, remembers Frank as "one of the nicest boys I ever met. He never rebelled at an order and he applied himself hard. He was just fooling around with the idea of being a sports writer, but I think he would have made a good one if he had wanted to continue with it."

But young Sinatra never wanted to be anything but a singer. He sang on the Hoboken sidewalks in the evenings, often with the ukulele his uncle Dom had given him for his fifteenth birthday. He sang at beach parties and on summer holidays with relatives. In high school, he took on the job of hiring the musicians for the school dances and got to know many of the local bands. Once in a while, he'd sing a number with them.

"He just seemed like a bag of bones in a padded jacket," a school friend recalled. "But he was already making the girls turn around and watch him. He had a kind of style."

One of the girls who was especially attracted to him was Nancy Barbato, daughter of a plasterer, whom he met at one of the Italian family gatherings.

One evening in 1933, Frank and his then-fiancée, Nancy, went to the Loewe's Journal Square Theater in Jersey City to hear Bing Crosby. "The Groaner" was Number One then, successor to the throne of Rudy Vallee, the throat throb of the 1920s.

When the 18-year-old Sinatra left the theater, he announced his life-long intention: "I'm going to be a singer." He quit his newspaper job and went after his goal, undeterred by the fact that he couldn't read a note of music. He told his parents his plans; they humored him, but kept hoping he would go into business instead; at the least they hoped that he would go on to college.

Once, Dolly came home to find a photograph of Bing Crosby in Frank's room. She threw a shoe at her son.

"My old man thought that anyone who wanted to go into the music business must be a bum," Sinatra recalled years later. "Bum" or no, the young man had his sights set on singing—and on Broadway.

He started out with a second-hand portable public address system—Dolly helped him buy it—and went around to ballrooms and local clubs, playing as many dates as he could at three dollars a gig. He joined amateur units, a regular feature of vaudeville at the time, and he entered amateur contests, winning one in a local Jersey City theater and going on to another in New York.

He latched on to a Hoboken trio who called themselves "The Three Flashes," Jim Petrozelli, Pat Principe, and Fred Tamburro. The group was asked by a local promoter to make some tests for the Major Bowes Amateur Hour, the most popular and influential of the talent shows, and Frank pressured them to let him join. He was made the lead singer within a week and was the main attraction when they auditioned for Major Bowes.

First broadcast in 1927, the Amateur Hour assembled talented fledgling performers from all over the country to compete against each other for top honors. "The wheel of fortune goes round and round," emcee and originator Major Edward Bowes would say. "And where it stops nobody knows." It stopped for Sinatra at the Capitol Theater on September 8, 1935. (It was

The year is 1935. Sinatra (R.) is 19. And his first singing engagements were with a group called the Hoboken Four, which performed on radio's "Amateur Hour," hosted by Major Bowes (C.) Others in the group were Fred Tamburro, Jimmy Petrozelli, and Pat Principe.

to stop for many other talented people, including Robert Merrill, Vera-Ellen, and Vic Damone, who also made their first nationwide appearances on "The Amateur Hour.")

Bowes renamed the Flashes "The Hoboken Four." The show was picked up by a local radio station and was well enough received for the Major to sign them up as a road attraction. Sinatra's salary was $50 a week, plus meals. But he soon tired of it, seeing it as a road to nowhere, and he returned to New Jersey to play the clubs and dance halls again. He ended up singing on several

continuing New Jersey radio programs. At one point in 1939, he was singing on 18 radio shows; his take-home pay was 70 cents, paid as carfare by one of the stations.

Discouraged, he quit to take a job as headwaiter in a New Jersey roadhouse for $15, then $25, a week. On this salary, he married Nancy at Our Lady of Sorrows Church in Jersey City, on February 4, 1939. They had a three-day honeymoon.

The Rustic Cabin was a local roadhouse on Route 9W near Alpine, New Jersey. It was there that the hard-working and single-minded

Sinatra got a job as master of ceremonies, headwaiter, and sometime singer. More important, the Cabin music was picked up by local radio stations and was eventually hooked up as a regular radio feature.

A former trumpeter in Benny Goodman's band, named Harry James, heard the music from the Cabin on radio one night when it was broadcast on WNEW's "Dance Parade."

James, who had started his own band and was looking for a vocalist, liked what he heard and called the station for the singer's name. He stopped by the Rustic Cabin to hear Sinatra the next night and signed him at $75 a week. On June 30, Sinatra appeared with the Harry James band on their first tour stop, the Hippodrome Theater in Baltimore. He toured with the band for six months before it broke up.

(c.1942). Sinatra rehearsing with Harry James for a radio broadcast. James "discovered" the young singer when he was performing at the Rustic Cabin, a local New Jersey roadhouse.

From there they went on to the Roseland Ballroom in Manhattan, where they played through the summer. Reviewers were beginning to comment on the singer's "pleasing vocals" and "easy phrasing." In Chicago, they played the Hotel Sherman, and Sinatra got some significant notices of a different kind. One reviewer said his vocal interpretations were not very convincing. Later, in a *Down Beat* magazine article, a conversation was recorded between the interviewer and Harry James:

"Who's that skinny little singer?" the journalist asked. "He sings a great song."

"Not so loud," James answered. "The kid's name is Sinatra. He considers himself the greatest vocalist in the business. No one ever heard of him. He looks like a wet rag. But he says he's the greatest. If he hears you compliment him, he'll ask for a raise."

He had not yet made a recording, but that was soon to change. On July 13, 1939, 24-year-old Frank Sinatra entered the recording studios for the first time, with the Harry James orchestra. The young vocalist didn't even have a credit on the record label; he was still just another performer. He sang "From the Bottom of My Heart," with "All or Nothing at All" on the flip side.

Years later, Sinatra would talk about the significance of that first recording. He told biographer Robin Douglas-Home: "You can never do anything in life quite on your own. I suppose you might be able to write a poem or paint a picture entirely on your own, but I doubt it. I don't think you can ever sing a song that way, anyhow.

"Yet, in a sort of paradoxical way, making a record is as near as you can get to it—although, of course, the arranger and the orchestra play an enormous part. But once you're on that record singing, it's you and it's you alone. If it's bad and gets criticized, it's you who's to blame—no one else. If it's good, it's also you."

Sinatra played for six months with Harry James and his orchestra, recording "My Buddy" and "These Are the Things I Love" (which are on the CBS album, "The Essential Frank Sinatra"), as well as the one song which became identified with him throughout his long career: "All or Nothing at All." It was his first big hit, even though it sold only 8,000 copies

that year. By 1943, when Sinatra had become a star, Columbia Records re-released it and it hit the million-record mark.

When Sinatra and the James band played the Sherman Hotel in Chicago, Jimmy Hilliard of CBS was there for the opening session in the Panther Room. He remembers: "My back was to the bandstand, but when the kid started talking a chorus, I had to turn around. I couldn't resist going back the next night to hear him again." Hilliard told Tommy Dorsey about the young singer. The rumor was that Dorsey's vocalist, Jack Leonard (of "Marie" fame) wanted to go out on his own, and Sinatra knew it.

After six months on the road, the Harry James orchestra folded. Sinatra had had a two-year contract, with time yet to run on it. But, when Dorsey came along and offered the singer $100 a week, James didn't object. Quite the contrary. "Nancy was expecting a baby and Frank needed the money and I wasn't going to stand in his way." The band wasn't doing too well, either.

Sinatra recalls that parting: "When I told Harry about Tommy's offer and said I wanted to leave, he just tore up my contract then and there and wished me luck. That night the bus pulled out with the rest of the boys at about half-past midnight. I'd said goodbye to them all and it was snowing, I remember. There was nobody around and I stood along with my suitcase in the snow and watched the tail lights disappear. Then the tears started and I tried to run after the bus. There was such spirit and enthusiasm in that band. I hated leaving it."

Sinatra admits he learned almost everything he knows about music from his time with Dorsey. He noted that Dorsey's success was largely due to his way of "phrasing with the horn," and Frank set about trying to do the same thing with his voice. Later, a couple of musical associates analyzed Sinatra's singing secret as his way of tying "phrases together with moans," using a practiced trick of breathing in the middle of a note so he can continue a lyric without a detectable break for breath. This is only a partial explanation, of course. Others have commented on his intimate way of singing—"I am a bedroom singer," Frank once said—and on his lyric sensitivity, as well as on his youthful, appealing boyishness.

Reunion at the Paramount with Tommy Dorsey, prior to
their stage show. August, 1956.

Sinatra's first concert appearance with the Dorsey group—which included singer Connie Haines, who had moved with him from Harry James' band; the Pied Pipers; and vocalist Jo Stafford—was in Rockford, Illinois, in January, 1940. There was one other important person in the group: the Norwegian arranger, Axel Stordahl. This was a name, and a talent, that was to accompany and encourage the young singer through many of those early years.

Between 1940 and 1942, Sinatra made 84 recordings with Dorsey's orchestra, some with the Pied Pipers. Among the first was "I'll Never Smile Again," which quickly jumped to the top of the charts. It stayed there for seven weeks. Some of the others were: "Street of Dreams," "There Are Such Things," "Stardust," "Let's Get Away from It All," and "This Love of Mine."

And there was another first, a daughter: Nancy Sandra Sinatra, born June 8, 1940: "Nancy with the Laughing Face."

"Daddy" Sinatra needed to work harder now and Dorsey certainly provided the opportunities. The band took part in a film, *Las Vegas Nights*—surely an ironic title for Sinatra's first Hollywood appearance—for Paramount, in which Frank sang "Dolores" and "I'll Never Smile Again," appearing only as the male soloist with the orchestra. It was a simple little story of a troupe of entertainers in that infamous gambling town, and starred Constance Moore and Bert Wheeler.

They tried again with an MGM release, *Ship Ahoy*, with Eleanor Powell, Red Skelton, Bert Lahr, and Virginia O'Brien. Frank sang "On Moonlight Bay," "The Last Call for Love,"

Frank and Nancy with their three-year-old daughter (also Nancy), August, 1943.

and "Poor You," and got some individual mentions in the reviews: " . . . Frank Sinatra, doing 90 percent of the vocalizing in the film, and doing it well, stands out," said one critic.

Meanwhile, the band was playing both major engagements and one-nighters, traveling from New York's Paramount to the Hollywood Palladium, from the Astor Roof to the Meadowbrook in New Jersey.

Earl Wilson, nationally syndicated entertainment columnist who was later to write his own biography of Sinatra, remembers going to the performance at the Meadowbrook.

"When we arrived, something extraordinary was happening around Dorsey's bandstand. Dorsey was famous for his dance music, but the young couples who came there to dance quit dancing when the boy singer sang. They clustered around the bandstand, hand in hand or arms around each other, and I looked up at him as he sang.

"He was something I hadn't seen before. My wife, who was only a few years older than Sinatra and had already heard him sing, was rolling her eyes and saying things like, 'Woo, woo!' "

"Sexy" was the way many of his young fans described him, as he stood, seemingly supported by the microphone, wearing a dark suit which appeared much too big for him, usually a thin wool sweater—and a bowtie. He seemed like a little boy; the spit curl added to that image. Whatever it was, the attraction was real.

By the middle of 1941, he had worked his way from twenty-second on the previous year's charts to the top of the *Billboard* College Music Poll of the young dance crowd. Soon he was to replace Bing Crosby, his boyhood idol, at the head of the *Down Beat* poll. With the help and guidance of arranger and conductor Stordahl, Sinatra made some solo recordings: "Night and Day," "The Night We Called it a Day," "The Song Is You," and "Lamplighter's Serenade."

Stordahl would later recall that recording session: "Frank had a room in the Hollywood Plaza on Vine Street. We sat in it all afternoon of a sunny day playing the two sides [of the advance dubs] over and over on a portable machine. Frank just couldn't believe his ears. He was so excited.

"I think that was a turning point in his career. I think he began to see what he might do on his own."

Sinatra was indeed thinking of going out on his own and, although it cost him a lot financially, he broke with the Dorsey band in September, 1942. Under the terms of the contract severance, Dorsey was to take one-third of Sinatra's future earnings and Dorsey's manager, Leonard Vannerson, another ten percent. A year later, and when he was in a much better financial position, Sinatra moved over to new agents at the Music Corporation of America (MCA), who helped him buy out of that contract—for more than $50,000.

"They held an option on me when I quit the Dorsey band," Sinatra reported, "and they wouldn't let me go unless I signed the contract. Dorsey is a good guy, and I learned a lot from him, but I thought that giving him one-third of my earnings for the next ten years was a pretty high price to pay. So I didn't pay. He sued me.

"I can tell you, this is a big load off my shoulders," he said when the settlement was announced.

Out on his own, Sinatra made a deal with CBS Radio and got a big buildup from them. He had two radio shows, one half-hour and one 15-minute program at first, then 15 minutes across the board at 11:15 at night. He signed a Columbia Records contract to record solo, and he lured Stordahl away from Dorsey to do the arranging. Dorsey had been paying Stordahl $150 a week; Sinatra gave him $650.

Then he made a deal to sing on American Tobacco's "Lucky Strike Hit Parade," replacing Barry Wood. "Hit Parade" presented the most popular song hits of the week in order of their popularity, with the Number One tune always sung last. Some songs remained popular for as many as 20 weeks, so they were arranged musically in different ways to give the show some variety. Lucky Strike "extras," old but favorite tunes, also broke up the monotony.

Sinatra did a three-minute spot singing "Night and Day" for a Columbia Pictures movie, *Reveille with Beverly*. He returned from Hollywood to get a twice-weekly radio slot on CBS (with the help of Columbia Records' Manny Sachs) called "Songs by Sinatra." Sachs also encouraged him to seek

Rita Stearns, a 17-year-old, Washington, D.C., high school girl, won an essay contest in which she described "The Voice" thus: "If lonesome, he reminds you of the guy away from your arms. If waiting for a Dream Prince, his thrilling voice sings for you alone." For these profound observations, Miss Stearns won the priviledge of being an audience-of-one for a Sinatra CBS nationwide broadcast. January 5, 1944.

representation with General Artists Corporation, MCA's biggest rival.

The manager of the Paramount Theater, Robert Weitman, prodded by Sinatra's agent at GAC, Harry Romm, went to hear Sinatra at the Mosque Theater in Newark, New Jersey. He recalled: "This skinny kid walks out on the stage. He wasn't much older than the kids in the seats. As soon as they saw him, they went crazy. And when he started to sing, they stood up and yelled and moaned and carried on until I thought—you should excuse the expression— his pants had fallen down."

Weitman persuaded Benny Goodman to take the young singer on as an "Extra Added Attraction" for the Paramount's post-Christmas show, opening December 30, 1942. It was there, as soon as the curtains opened to the introduction of "Frank Sinatra," that a new era of entertainment began. One historian recalled it this way:

"A girl in the twelfth row fainted—or 'swooned.' Another girl, startled, stood up and screamed. No one knows exactly what happened in the next few seconds, but Sinatra continued to sing . . . By the time he had finished, the theater was a charivari, with every girl in the theater on her feet, shrieking. The screeching spread like a plague.

"He became known as the Voice. Wherever the Voice appeared, pandemonium followed. Autograph hunters chased him through drugstores, restaurants, department stores, and his home. They climbed his roof to peer into his bedroom. If he walked in mud, they dug up the earth in an effort to preserve his footprints."

On the program with him at the Paramount (which was playing the film, *Star Spangled Rhythm*) were Peggy Lee, the Radio Rogues, and Moke & Poke. Variety wrote:

"Frank Sinatra, ex-Tommy Dorsey vocalist, now on his own and due to step into Lucky Strike's 'Hit Parade' soon, rates as the outstanding click of the bill. Despite an apparent nervousness in his voice this show, he hit the customers solidly with 'Where or When,' 'There Are Such Things,' 'Craziest Dreams,' 'For Me and My Gal,' and 'The Song Is You.' He sells tunes easily and he possesses a wealth of smooth salesmanship in his voice, phrasing and shading perfectly. Here's a definite comer as a soloist.''

The combination of critical acclaim and audience adoration made Sinatra more than a comet on the rise; he was an immediate phenomenon.

The gate at the Paramount set a record daily: $15,000 or so the first Wednesday night; $30,000 the next; an estimated $115,000 for the first seven nights; actually $113,500 through New Year's Eve, the highest box office take in the Paramount's 16 years of operation.

The teenage girls of the land, relatively well-integrated members of the American scene until then, suddenly erupted as a screaming, fanatical mass. Nothing like it had been seen before. And Sinatra knew then that he had made the right decision to go out on his own.

Years later, speaking of that Paramount engagement, he was to tell Bob Thomas, Hollywood correspondent for *The Associated Press:* "They tore the joint down. That was the first I knew I could make the grade. I had always held the thought that I could go back to Dorsey if I didn't make good. It was wonderful. But it was hectic. I never really had time to sit down and think about where I was going. I just enjoyed it."

Was he ever really hurt by the young mobs?

By 1943, the bobbysoxers were already in a swoon over the skinny new singing sensation. These young ladies are losing their hearts at a Hollywood Bowl concert.

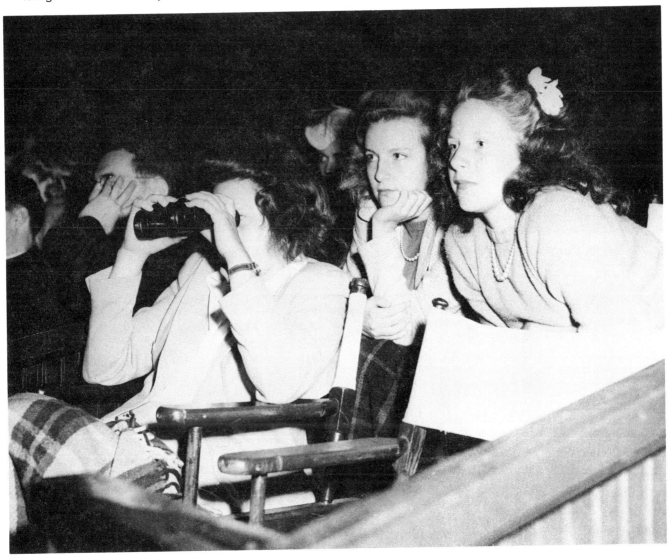

Besieged in Pasadena, August, 1943, prior to a
Hollywood Bowl concert.

"No, not really. That part was blown up by
reporters; it made for colorful writing, but it
wasn't really true. The kids would grab for a
handkerchief; that was standard. But I never
had them tear the clothes off me. Occasionally,
I would have a torn lapel when they tried to
grab me.

"I remember once I arrived at an airport in
Toronto, or Quebec, and a big guy decided he
wanted my trench coat for a souvenir. He tried
to grab it off my arm and I wasn't about to part

with it. We had a real tug-of-war.. Luckily, a
cop came along and saved me, because the
guy was pretty big.

"There was only once I was really hurt. I
had finished singing in the Wedgewood Room
of the Waldorf-Astoria and had to go back to
the radio studio to do the West Coast repeat of
the 'Hit Parade.' As I walked out of the door, a
freak thing happened. Two guys grabbed for
my bowtie and they got both ends. Neither
would let go and I was backed against a wall

gasping for breath. I nearly went under before George Evans [his press agent] saved me. There was a big crease around my neck for weeks afterward. I had to have massages to get rid of it."

How much of the bobbysox buildup was real and how much was publicity?

"It was all real. It started when I was with Tommy Dorsey's band. When I went out on my own, I hired George Evans to try and hold down the publicity. I was afraid it was getting out of hand. We didn't have to dream up anything; it was all there."

Testament to that comes from Frank Capra, Hollywood director who, in 1944, hadn't yet met Sinatra. Capra, then making films for the Army, was home on leave and arrived in Los Angeles on the same train. As he recalls in his autobiography: "I saw a large crowd outside the [Super] Chief as we slowed to a stop at the Los Angeles station. How nice, I thought, they're here to cheer Major Bong [air ace of the Pacific and Medal of Honor winner, also on the train].

"I saw Major Bong walk unnoticed through the welcoming crowd of chattering teenagers, mostly girls. A mass scream scared the daylights out of me. Frank Sinatra stood in the Pullman car waving at his frenzied fans.

"Was Frank Sinatra an omen of an instinctive change in human females? Was motherhood's age-old wisdom whispering intuitive instructions to these frenetic teenagers: 'Girls, war is for the dodo bird. Give the brush-off to bemedaled heroes who boast of killing and violence. Let the fathers of your sons be gentle peace heroes who sing of sex sweet sex and the bluebird.' "

Everyone—fans and detractors alike—tried to explain it, tried to understand it. Psychiatry, then a minor medical discipline, had a field day: "A maternal urge to feed the hungry;"

Hollywood: the police have to hold back the girls at this concert in August, 1943. Amateur psychiatrists tried to explain Sinatra's appeal. Some claimed it was wartime degeneracy, others the maternal instinct he engendered as he crooned his lyrics while idly fondling his wedding ring. Whatever it was, the girls went crazy.

Sinatra signs up for the draft in Newark, New Jersey, on December 9, 1943. At R., Mrs. Mae E. Jones, the Draft Board chief clerk. Frank was given a 4-F classification because of a perforated left eardrum.

A year after signing up for the draft, Frank reports again (Jersey City, New Jersey, February 8, 1945) for a second eligibility physical. He was again given a 4-F rating.

Bobbysoxers bid farewell to Sinatra (and Phil Silvers at his R.) as he prepares to leave on a USO tour to entertain the troops overseas. March, 1945.

"Mass frustrated love;" "It's as if he had musk glands instead of vocal cords;" and, finally, "He's just about the only male left around."

Indeed, he was—just about. The Army tried to change that, but finally ended up classifying him 4-F in a Newark induction center because of punctured eardrums, apparently incurred during one of several mastoid operations he'd had as a child. Sinatra announced how disappointed he was at that decision: "I've been bragging to friends that I'd get through."

In fact, he tried to have the classification changed and wound up 2-A, a special classification putting him in an activity "in support of the national health, safety or interests." It allowed him to pursue his new-found success with fervor and freedom. And he did.

Offers from radio and from Hollywood followed as a matter of course. He had shown he was more than an "Extra Added Attraction." He was The Attraction. At least among young teenage girls.

With the single-mindedness, shrewdness, and ambition which had brought him this far, Sinatra set out to show he could lure the adult crowd, too. That meant playing the New York clubs.

With Frances Langford and Bing Crosby rehearsing for the annual "Command Performance" held by the Armed Forces Radio Service, September 23, 1945.

But the only place which would take him on, at the insistence of his GAC agent, Harry Kilbyk, was the Riobamba Club, which was on the verge of closing because of money troubles. It was a whole new gig when he opened at the East 57th Street club at $750 a week—once again as an "Extra Added Attraction." And once again, he proved he could do it.

The night club audiences, adults, couples, loved him,—especially the women. During Sinatra's ten weeks at the Riobamba, the place was packed every night. His fee went from $750 a week to $1,000, then to $1,500. "What his singing does to women is immoral," said one male customer. "But it's pleasant," he added.

He returned for a time to the Meadowbrook in New Jersey, then came triumphantly back to the Paramount, for $2,500 a week. After that, he played the Wedgewood Room at the Waldorf and was tagged "the hottest thing in show biz." A series of concerts were arranged by press agent George Evans, with the New York Philharmonic, the National Symphony in Washington, D.C., the Cleveland Symphony, and the Hollywood Bowl Orchestra. "Your Hit Parade" had doubled its audience since Sinatra made his debut on it. Hollywood wanted him. He was on his way to his first million dollars.

He had the world on a string.

Rehearsing for his radio show, 1947.

At an outdoor mall concert in Los Angeles, June 29, 1943.

At a recording session in December, 1947. The American Federation of Musicians was about to strike the radio broadcasting industry at the end of year and, in an attempt to beat the deadline, Sinatra made 75 records in a two-month period.

The 1940s proved to be the dazzling decade for young Sinatra; it brought out the best—and probably the worst—in him. With the plugging and prodding of close friends and advisers like Manny Sachs of Columbia Records, who was important in Sinatra's early breaks as a recording soloist, and friend and adviser Hank Sanicola, Sinatra became a welcome attraction wherever he performed: in clubs, recording studios, or in Hollywood.

Columbia had signed him to a seven-year recording contract in 1943, a 16-song agreement for a mere $1,600 advance. Less than two years later, he had a new contract and, by 1948, a third contract gave him $6,000 a month advance money. "All or Nothing at All"—which became a virtual theme song—had made the top of the "Hit Parade," as did his recording of "You'll Never Know." "People Will Say We're in Love" and "Sunday, Monday or Always" made it soon after.

Sinatra, Sanicola, and music publisher Ben Barton went into business as Barton Music. This was Sinatra's first venture into the financial side of music. They acquired "Put Your Dreams Away," "Close to You," Sammy Cahn's

"Saturday Night Is the Loneliest Night in the Week," and Jimmy Van Heusen's "Nancy with the Laughing Face," with lyrics by comedian Phil Silvers.

Live on stage—where he most enjoyed performing—Sinatra played the Copacabana and soon topped Jimmy Durante as New York's top club attraction. Durante once talked movie director Frank Capra into catching Sinatra at a late-night show at the Copa. As Capra recalls it in his autobiography:

"I heard him grab that late-night audience; heard him grab me. He knew the meaning of his lyrics and sang them to you, powerfully, dramatically. Vocal cords swelling out from his thin neck, face contorted with passion, blue eyes moist with meaning—that thin, vibrant man sang like nobody of his time, like nobody of today. Durante introduced us in his dressing room. I mumbled something like, 'Boy, you've got it. Don't throw it away. . . .' "

Capra and Sinatra were to get together years later, combining talents for the movie *A Hole in the Head.*

Sinatra returned to the Paramount Theater, scene of his first real triumph, and topped it. This was in October, 1944 and became known as the "Columbus Day Riot." Before dawn on that day, bobbysoxers, ignoring a nine o'clock curfew set by New York's Mayor Fiorello

The famous "Columbus Day Riot," October 12, 1944. Police estimated that at Sinatra's holiday concert at New York City's Paramount, 25,000 teenage fans stormed the theater.

LaGuardia, were out in force. So were the police, who estimated that some 10,000 youngsters had taken advantage of the school holiday to see Sinatra. Or to try to. The line extended a whole block around 43rd and 44th Streets and Eighth Avenue. Thousands of others roamed the Times Square area. When the doors finally opened, the box office was crushed and nearby shop windows were shattered.

The Commissioner of the Board of Education, George Chatfield, accused Sinatra of contributing to truancy: "We don't want this sort of thing to go on. We cannot tolerate young people making a public display of losing control of their emotions."

Sinatra took Hollywood by a similar storm.

He went out to Tinsel Town to discuss the possibility of a job as staff singer on NBC's Hollywood-based radio show. Instead, he got the chance to sing "Night and Day" in a Columbia musical, *Reveille with Beverly,* with Ann Miller as a tap-dancing disc jockey.

RKO Pictures signed him for *Higher and Higher,* which was based on the play by Gladys Hurlbut and Joshua Logan, with original music by Rodgers and Hart. Sinatra got co-star billing, after Michele Morgan and Jack Haley. (Frank doesn't get the girl; Haley does.) Songwriter Jimmy McHugh, who was selected by RKO to be Sinatra's "official host," composed the songs for the film, along with Harry Adamson. McHugh was to become a lifelong friend.

Frank sang "You Belong in a Love Song,"

Another view of Sinatra's 1944 Paramount concert.

With Gloria DeHaven in *Step Lively,* 1945. Frank decided, after shooting this scene, that "the movies are a great art medium."

"I Couldn't Sleep a Wink Last Night," (which won an Academy Award nomination), "A Lovely Way to Spend an Evening," "The Music Stopped," and "I Saw You First." And Sinatra as an actor? Said the *Los Angeles Times* critic: "He plays himself in *Higher and Higher,* appears more at ease than we expected, and should find his place as a film personality with careful choice of subjects. Crosby did it, didn't he?"

Sinatra played himself in most of his early movies, which was exactly what RKO wanted when it signed him to a seven-year contract, following the gratifying returns on the film *Step Lively*—a musical remake of the Marx brothers' *Room Service.* Sinatra, at the height of his popularity, got top billing and sang several songs by Jule Styne and Sammy Cahn, including "Come Out, Come Out, Wherever You Are," "Then You Kissed Me," and "As Long As There's Music." "Sinatra's name on the marquee," *Time* magazine opined, "is sufficient to guarantee lipsticky posters on the outside, moaning galleryites within."

It was also enough to persuade Louis B. Mayer to buy Sinatra's RKO contract and place his name among those in the "Studio of the Stars." His first film for MGM was *Anchors Aweigh* and, although he is outshined by choreographer-dancer-actor Gene Kelly, it is a delightful film, beautifully played by all. (A memorable dance sequence, featuring Kelly and the animated mouse, Jerry—from the "Tom and Jerry" cartoons—was enough to make *Anchors Aweigh* a near-classic.)

In 1945, the year *Anchors Aweigh* was released, Sinatra showed yet another facet of his complex and sometimes contradictory personality. He helped produce, and starred in, a ten-minute short film against racial and religious intolerance: *The House I Live In.* Mervyn LeRoy directed it and Albert Maltz wrote the script. At the Oscar presentations that year, Sinatra received a wonderful personal welcome. *The House I Live In* was awarded a special Oscar.

Ironically, the kudos Sinatra received for *The House I Live In*—the title song became a

Hollywood, March 11, 1946. Frank and wife Nancy attend the Oscar celebrations at Ciros. Earlier in the evening, Sinatra's film, *The House I Live In,* received a special award.

standard part of his repertoire—were somewhat dampened by a misguided effort in his next film, *Till the Clouds Roll By*. In that movie biography of Jerome Kern, Frank sings "Ol' Man River" ludicrously dressed in a white tuxedo and standing on a white pedestal.

Albert Maltz, incidentally, was to figure prominently in a later controversy involving Sinatra. Frank had acquired the film rights to *The Execution of Private Slovik*, William Bradford Huie's WW II book about the only American to be shot for desertion since the Civil War. He hired Maltz to write the screenplay. But it was 1960, and Maltz was on the Hollywood blacklist, accused of Communist sympathies.

Sinatra, a tolerant man, perhaps one of the most courageous in Hollywood, tried to fight it. He withstood attacks from the press; from the American Legion; from John Wayne, movieland's ultra-right-wing representative. There was pressure put on disc jockeys not to play Sinatra's records. He got no support from friends or associates. Finally, he gave in, fired Maltz, and sold the film rights to George Stevens.

By this time, Sinatra had reached a point of popularity at which it was easy to recognize when others parodied him—a sure sign of his success. In a dreamy version of "That Old Black Magic," for instance, in the movie *Here Come the Waves*, it's his buddy Bing Crosby who satirizes "The Swooner" and his bobbysox worshippers.

In all his early films, Sinatra played on his popularity as a singer and his easygoing, charming manner on the screen.

In *It Happened in Brooklyn*, he teamed up with Kathryn Grayson, Peter Lawford, and Jimmy Durante, and sang Styne-Cahn tunes like "Time After Time," and (with Durante), "The Song's Gotta Come from the Heart" (a perfect title for a Sinatra tune).

In *The Miracle of the Bells*, he played with Fred MacMurray and Alida Valli, and sang "Ever Homeward," by Styne, Cahn, and Kasimierz Lubomirski.

But by the late forties, that popularity started to diminish, and so did his movie allure, for audiences and filmmakers alike. *The Kissing Bandit*, a musical romance, which also starred Kathryn Grayson, may well have been the

nadir, with Sinatra, in costume, playing a womanizing desperado. It was awful, a fact Sinatra never disputed.

The last two films he did for MGM, in 1948 and 1949, were really Gene Kelly vehicles: *Take Me Out to the Ball Game* and *On the Town*. The pair appeared as baseball-playing vaudevillians in the former, with Esther Williams and Jules Munshin. Sinatra soloed "The Right Girl for Me." But most memorable was "O'Brien to Ryan to Goldberg," with Kelly and Munshin. In *On the Town*, the trio of Sinatra-Kelly-Munchin was aided by Vera-Ellen, Betty Garrett, and Ann Miller. It introduced the song "New York, New York," which Frank did with Kelly and Munshin, and which quickly became a Sinatra standard.

The forties' fame brought fortune, too. And Frank was generous with his gains, then, as later. He gave away $250 Dunhill lighters, which became something of a trademark. He also made more significant charitable offerings, which he tried to do as anonymously as possible. "Perhaps," said one friend, "Frank is the wildest spender of modern times. He throws it around like a drunken admiral." He once financed a $5,000 wedding for a friend. In another year, he supposedly spent more than $30,000 on last-minute Christmas gifts.

In 1943, he and Nancy moved into a house in Hasbrouck Heights, New Jersey. It had a sort of Dutch colonial entrance and a Cape Cod bay window. They planned for a tennis court in the back, a movie projector hidden in the sun porch wall, and a loudspeaker in the fireplace. Then, when he won the West, he bought a $250,000 home in exclusive Holmby Hills and another, for $162,000, in the Palm Springs desert.

Barbara Stanwyck, who lived close by, became a good friend. So did neighbor Humphrey Bogart and his wife, Lauren Bacall. The Sinatras, Bogart, Bacall, restaurateur Mike Romanoff, and a bunch of other Hollywood nonconformists would gather in the Bogart den, which became the liveliest place in town. Indeed, at a time when newspapers were writing about juvenile gangs that preyed on the Los Angeles area, Lauren Bacall suggested:

"I think we should call this bunch of adult delinquents 'The Holmby Hills Rat Pack.' "

The name stuck.

Frank joins his long-time friend for "Gene Kelly . . . An American in Pasadena," broadcast on CBS-TV, March 13, 1978.

At the premiere of *The Miracle of the Bells,* with master of ceremonies, Harry Crocker. Hollywood, May 12, 1948.

Frank sits for the noted American sculptor, Jo Davidson (a sign of the singer's growing popularity, since Davidson specialized in famous "heads"). November, 1947.

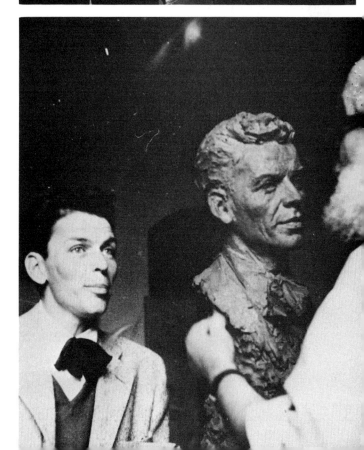

24

While it flourished in those dazzling years of Sinatra's early success, the Rat Pack was as exclusive as Park Avenue's 400. "Prince" Mike Romanoff said it was even more exclusive: "After all, one can be born into the 400. The Holmby Hills' Rat Pack picks its own."

Bogart used to say that Sinatra was "head rat." But Frank replied that the title belonged to Bogie. "It was his booze," he said.

Sinatra's parties, too, were legend. Champagne and women were never lacking at a Sinatra bash. Sometimes more women than champagne (or, more likely, Jack Daniels sour mash). One story has a friendly female fan asking for an autograph on her bra. Another tells of a woman who walked into Sinatra's room wearing a mink coat. Only a mink coat.

Hollywood's reputation always has been closer to Babylon—if not Sodom—than to Peoria or Pittsburgh. Sinatra certainly kept the image alive and kicking.

He was seen, early, and late, and often, with Lana Turner, with Marilyn Maxwell, with Gloria Vanderbilt, with Anita Ekberg. And, later,

Part of "The Rat Pack" at Hollywood's Copa Room, October 19, 1956. (L. to R.): Humphrey Bogart (or the back of his head); producer Sid Luft; Lauren Bacall; Judy Garland; Ellie Graham; agent Jack Entratter; restaurateur Mike Romanoff (partly hidden); Sinatra; Mrs. Romanoff; actor David Niven and his wife.

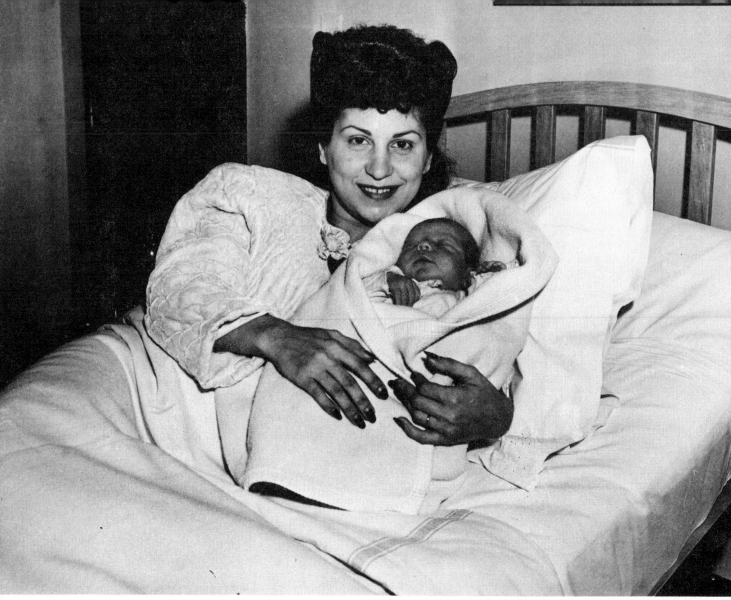

Nancy Sinatra with newborn son, Franklin Wayne (Frank Jr.)—named after President Roosevelt. November 1, 1944.

Sinatra being fingerprinted by Deputy Sheriff Bob Rogers in Los Angeles when he applied for a gun permit. The singer says he needs it for protection because of the late hours he keeps. January 30, 1947.

with Marilyn Monroe, Lady Adele Beatty, Dorothy Provine, and Jill St. John. And with a bunch of lesser-known, but equally beautiful starlets—and star-nots.

"I like broads," Frank allowed over the years. But he once told a reporter: "If I did half of what they say, I wouldn't be here—I'd be in a jar at Harvard."

Nancy, of course, was well aware of the reports of her husband's late-night carousing—and of his long absences from home. But there was daughter Nancy, young Franklin Wayne—named after Franklin D. Roosevelt, but always known as Frank Jr.—born January 10, 1944, and Christina (Tina), who arrived June 20, 1948. After a brief separation, there was the widely-circulated story of a reconciliation, when Frank and Nancy met "accidentally" at comedian Phil Silvers' opening night at Slapsie Maxies in Hollywood. Sinatra appeared as an invitation artist and sang "Going Home." When he finished, Silvers led him over to Nancy's table for a touching embrace.

The Sinatras at the Oscars, Hollywood, October 6, 1946. (Unknown to the public, the couple was living apart at the time.)

October 23, 1946. Separated for several weeks, Frank and Nancy meet accidentally, and are photographed together at a Hollywood night club. Shortly thereafter, they anounced their reconciliation.

Then came Ava Gardner.

Ava Lavinia Gardner was born December 24, 1922, on a farm in Smithfield, North Carolina, though her family moved to Newport News, Virginia, when she was 12. It was on the farm that she got into the habit of walking barefoot, something she continued to do as an adult, especially at Hollywood parties. She was a skinny, insecure little girl, but she developed into a sultry beauty and, as an actress, became the cinematic incarnation of the restless *femme fatale*.

Photographs of her, taken by her brother-in-law when she was eighteen, led to an MGM screen test and a $50-a-week contract as a starlet. She played her share of ingenue roles, posed for cheesecake publicity photos, and took lessons in acting and grooming.

She met and married Mickey Rooney, who was then shooting the Andy Hardy series on the MGM lot. The marriage lasted 20 months; they were divorced in 1943. After dating millionaire recluse Howard Hughes for three

Frank with Ava Gardner at the Ezzard Charles/Joe Louis fight in New York's Yankee Stadium, September 27, 1950.

years or so, she met oft-married bandleader Artie Shaw, whom she married on October 17, 1945. After one year, during which Ava had a nervous breakdown, they were divorced.

Meanwhile, she had appeared in *The Killers* with Burt Lancaster, *The Hucksters* with Clark Gable, and *One Touch of Venus,* in which she played a statue come to life. Supposedly, she sat for sculptor Josef Nicolosi in a two-piece bathing suit and, according to the publicity, removed the upper half for a touch of "realism."

Ava Gardner met Frank Sinatra at the premiere of *Gentlemen Prefer Blondes* in New York at the end of 1949 and saw him again at a Palm Springs party in January, 1950. They quickly became a press "item;" they were seen everywhere together, from Houston to New York, in Spain and England. It was the beginning of a stormy courtship—and marriage—which was to sizzle over several continents for more than five years.

"They were drawn to each other," wrote Miss Gardner's biographer, Charles Higham.

Ava Gardner hides in the back of the car from cameramen, as Frank tries to fend them off. The much-publicized pair had just arrived in Los Angeles after a six-day holiday in Mexico.

There was a sexual attraction, to be sure. There were also similar interests: both liked the night hours, Italian food, hard liquor, and boxing. They were both emotional and, at the same time, vulnerable.

Frank and Nancy Sinatra were legally separated in September, 1950. In a separate maintenance decree, granted by default in Superior Court in Santa Monica, California, Nancy won a third of her husband's annual income up to $150,000, plus ten percent of his income over that figure. And she got custody of their children. She had been living on $2,750-a-month support during negotiations over the property settlement. In addition to the gross income settlement, she got a 1950 Cadillac and the Holmby Hills mansion.

Frank kept a 1949 Cadillac and a jeep, the desert house in Palm Springs, and any phonograph records or radio transcripts he wanted. Also all the money in the bank accounts.

The divorce became official on October 30, 1951, under the terms of the separation agreement. In testimony at the divorce trial, there was no mention of Ava Gardner.

Nancy explained that Frank had told her his prolonged absences from home were because he was "out with the boys." Superior Court Judge Orlando H. Rhodes granted the divorce on grounds of cruelty. The settlement disclosed that Sinatra earned $367,000 from January 1 to August 31, 1951. That made Nancy's share roughly $72,000.

Nancy told columnist Louella Parsons at the time: "I refused him a divorce for a long time, because I thought he would come back to his home. I'm now convinced that a divorce is the only way to my happiness as well as Frank's."

At another time, she added: "No father could be more devoted or more kind to his family than Frank. And no family could love their father more." Indeed, they did stay the "best of friends" and Frank and his children were always close.

Frank (sporting a mustache) and Ava at the Riverside Hotel, Reno, Nevada, August 19, 1951. Sinatra was fulfilling a singing engagement, as well as the six-months residency requirement for a Nevada divorce.

California, September 28, 1950. Nancy Sinatra takes the witness stand. She is granted a decree of separate maintenance from the singer, under which she will receive approximately a third of her husband's income. Sinatra did not contest the action.

One day after Nancy divorced him, Frank made it official in Las Vegas, where there was no one-year waiting period for a final decree, as there was in California.

Frank Sinatra and Ava Gardner were married on November 7, at the suburban Philadelphia home of Lester Sachs, Manny's cousin. Axel Stordahl was best man.

But their impassioned disputes continued. One night in Reno, during their rambunctious romance, Frank reportedly took an overdose of sleeping pills. Another time, after a quarrel with Ava, he was admitted to a New York hospital with scratches on the lower part of his arm. On one especially raucous night in 1952, he threw Ava out of his house in Palm Springs.

Pennsylvania Station, New York. November 2, 1951. Frank and Ava arrive from Philadelphia, where they had quickly and quietly applied for a marriage license.

Cheek-to-cheek after the wedding.

On the 7th of November, 1951, in Philadelphia, Frank and Ava were married.

The newlyweds caught unawares on a lonely stretch of Miami beach the day after their wedding.

There were a number of stories, often disguised by his associates and publicists, that the on-again, off-again affair made Frank deeply despondent, if not suicidal. Certainly, he was nervous and unhappy and preoccupied with Ava during those troublesome years. His weight, never much to brag about on a 5-feet-11-inch frame, dropped from 132 to 118 pounds.

As if Ava weren't providing trauma enough, the government had placed a $250,000 tax lien against Frank's income. CBS canceled his television contract. For the first time since 1943, the *Down Beat* magazine poll did not have him among the top. (In 1949, Billy Eckstine headed the poll, followed by Frankie Laine, Bing Crosby, and Mel Torme.)

George Evans died suddenly early in 1950. Manny Sachs had resigned from Columbia Records and Mitch Miller had replaced him. Miller and Sinatra disagreed—a lot. That clash never was worked out. Columbia, noting the increasing popularity of singers Johnny Ray and Frankie Laine, and the decreasing interest in Frank Sinatra, let his contract expire. His last recording for Columbia was "Why Try to Change Me Now."

Sinatra also split with MGM on his movie contract, though it had several years to run. Howard Hughes hired him to co-star with Jane Russell and Groucho Marx in *Double Dynamite* (originally *It's Only Money*). But it didn't help. Only Groucho got good notices for this slight comedy, with critics noting: "Sinatra isn't called

Frank and Ava with Sinatra's parents, Dolly and Marty. November 14, 1951.

upon for any more than a haphazard performance." He did a Sinatra-like biography movie, *Meet Danny Wilson,* with Shelley Winters, about a brash but likable young crooner on his way to fame. One reviewer quipped: "The story cribs so freely from the career and personality of Frank Sinatra that fans may expect Ava Gardner to pop up in the last reel."

He fell out with his agents and with the press, which used phrases like "the last goodbye" and "the final indignity."

One night at the end of April, 1950, he was appearing at the Copa when he started to sing and "nothing came out but dust." He was unable to appear for the last two shows; Billy Eckstine went on for him. It turned out to be a throat hemorrhage, and Frank was ordered by his doctors to take a two-week rest—a silent treatment. But he preferred to stay at the apartment of Manny Sachs at the Gotham Hotel, in New York, where an oxygen tent was installed for his use.

It was the first time since his rise to fame that he had been seriously ill. It couldn't have helped his despondency much when few of his friends and associates came by with sympathy or aid.

An exception was Columbia studio boss Harry Cohn. In his biography, *King Cohn,* author Bob Thomas writes:

"Cohn flew to New York and spent the morning with Sinatra from 10 to 10:30. Cohn went off to business appointments and returned at 5 in the afternoon. He remained with Sinatra until his time for sleep at 9:30. Cohn read to his patient, reminisced of his early days in films, told jokes, and delivered numbers recalled from his days as a song plugger. Cohn continued the daily routine until Sinatra recovered."

Years later, Sinatra was to recall that period of abandonment: "Everybody deserted the

With Shelley Winters in *Meet Danny Wilson,* 1952.

ship, ran away, friends and people whose careers I'd helped, people from whom I never asked a dime or a dollar. They all deserted me, except one man, Jimmy Van Heusen. He called and asked what he could do.

"It was, for me, very disappointing. But I never got angry with them. When things got better, I went up to them all and greeted them. And they were astounded, wanted to back off a little, but I didn't give them a chance."

It was typical of the Sicilian Sinatra, who always remembered a friend—and one who wasn't.

When he returned to action after the throat problem, he announced: "I got away from a lot of things. I forgot work for a while. The pipes are okay again—I hope."

He returned, too, to the pursuit of unhappiness with Ava.

He appeared on Bob Hope's show and went to London to negotiate for a performance at the Palladium. Ava would be there.

He went off to Kenya, where Ava was shooting a movie called *Mogambo,* with Clark Gable. He drank with director John Ford, watched Gable and Gardner at work, and

Sinatra (waving in C.) greeted by fans at Blackpool, England, where he was taking a break from his London Palladium engagement. (July, 1950).

talked about a book he had read: *From Here to Eternity.*

The James Jones novel, *From Here to Eternity,* depicted the Army in Hawaii before the attack on Pearl Harbor, in harsh, raw, graphic terms. A secondary character in the book was Private Angelo Maggio, a quick-talking Italian from the city streets of the 1930s.

"I knew Maggio," Sinatra said of the character. "I went to high school with him in Hoboken. I was beaten up with him. I might have been Maggio," he imagined.

He wanted, desperately, to play Maggio.

Columbia studio head Harry Cohn had bought the film rights to the book for $82,000. No one else dared attempt to translate the rough, obscenity-filled text to film. Cohn hired Fred Zinneman to direct and wanted Eli Wallach to play Maggio. He signed Burt Lancaster, Montgomery Clift, Deborah Kerr, and Donna Reed for the leading roles. Sinatra pleaded for the part of Maggio.

Much has been said, written, and gossiped about how Sinatra finally got the role. A character in Mario Puzo's later best-selling book and film, *The Godfather,* was thinly disguised as a fictional down-on-his-luck singer who used mob connections to get a plum role. Others have suggested that it was Ava Gardner's personal prodding that got Frank a screen test with Cohn.

Bob Thomas, longtime *Associated Press* Hollywood correspondent, and author of Cohn's biography, describes what actually happened this way:

"Harry Cohn was unpersuaded by Sinatra's entreaties to be considered for the role of Maggio. Only when Ava Gardner made a personal plea to Cohn did he agree to test Sinatra. The singer flew from Nairobi to Hollywood at his own expense and sat outside Cohn's office for two hours before being admitted.

"I'll pay you if you let me play the role," said Sinatra.

He played two scenes for the screen test. "I was scared to death," he remembered later. "The next day I flew back to Africa, probably the longest trip an actor ever took for a 15-minute screen test."

Again, according to Bob Thomas: "His test proved impressive, but Sinatra had little hope

he would win the role; he had heard that Wallach was virtually cast for it. Then Wallach discovered the film conflicted with a commitment he had made with Elia Kazan to appear in *El Camino Real* on Broadway. Wallach declined the role of Maggio.

"Sinatra won it by default.

"Cohn offered Sinatra $1,000 a week for eight weeks, a fraction of what he'd previously earned in films. Sinatra and his agents agreed to the terms, especially since Cohn demanded no options on future pictures. They asked for assurance that Sinatra would be billed together with the other stars. It was a concession Cohn was reluctant to make, since he wanted to avoid any suggestion that *From Here to Eternity* was a musical. But, in the end, he billed all five stars above the title."

Sinatra worked hard on the role. Some said he was just playing himself; others saw the expression of a natural film talent.

From Here to Eternity, released in 1953, became the biggest money-maker in Columbia's history up to that time. It cost $2,400,000 to produce and returned $19,000,000 in its first release; it was later to make much, much more. All five leading players were nominated for Academy Awards.

The night before the Oscar presentations at the Pantages Theater on March 25, the Sinatra family, Nancy and the children, had a private supper party. They presented Frank with their own miniature Oscar, a religious medallion inscribed: "Dad, we'll love you—from here to eternity."

With Montgomery Cliff (L.) and Burt Lancaster in *From Here to Eternity.*

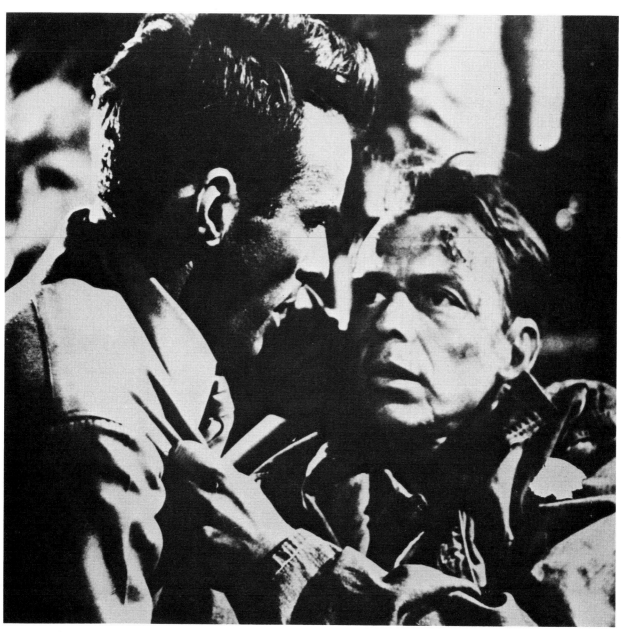

Sinatra as Maggio: the part he almost didn't get. His performance won him an Oscar.

Frank faced formidable opponents for that gold statuette: child actor Brandon DeWilde and Jack Palance, both in *Shane;* Eddie Albert in *Roman Holiday;* and Robert Strauss, in *Stalag 17.*

Sinatra attended the Awards affair with his son Frank Jr. and daughter Nancy. And when Mercedes McCambridge announced the Best Supporting Actor award to that glittering crowd, Sinatra sprinted to the stage and proclaimed breathlessly: "I am deeply thrilled and very moved." Laughingly he complained because "nobody asked me to sing."

Of course he had not sung a note in *From Here to Eternity* either; it was strictly a dramatic role.

Was the award a well-earned recognition of talent? Or was it a nostalgic recognition of past triumphs? Was it the result of pressure? Or a desire to get Frank back on his former professional footing?

The answer, resoundingly, was: recognition of talent. One critic called Sinatra's portrayal "memorable," and added: "There is no question about the excellence of the performance."

"He shocked the public," said another, "because he had never really reached them before. He was always a personality. Personalities come and go at regular intervals in the movie business, but the actors stay on. Cooper, Taylor, Gable, and several others were personalities before they proved themselves as actors."

The critic continued, "Sinatra, the actor, is exciting and unpredictable."

Time magazine oozed: "To the amazement of millions, the boudoir Johnny with the lotion tones stood revealed as a naturalistic actor of narrow but deep-cutting talents. He played what he is, the Kid from Hoboken, but he played him with rage and tenderness and grace, and he glinted in the barrel of human trash as poetically as an empty tin can in the light of a hobo's match."

In a retrospective letter, for publication in the "official history" of the Academy Awards, Sinatra recalled that big night.

"I've been up and down in my life more often than a roller coaster on the Fourth of July. At 38 years old, I was a has-been. Sitting by a phone that wouldn't ring. Wondering what happened to all the friends who grew invisible when the music stopped. Finding out fast how tough it is to borrow money when you're all washed up.

"Yes, when 1953 slid down the pole in Times Square, my only collateral was a dream. A dream to end my nightmare. And what a dream it was.

"It began when I dozed off after finishing an absolutely fascinating book written by a giant, James Jones. More than a book, it was a portrait of people I knew, understood, and could feel, and in it I saw myself as clearly as I see myself every morning when I shave. I was Maggio.

"No matter who said what, I was Maggio, and Maggio was I. And I would prove it, up there on the big screen. I would prove it no matter how many tests I was asked to make, nor what the money. I was going to become Maggio if it was the last thing I ever did.

"It was that gifted actress Mercedes McCambridge who woke me out of the dream. . . .

"Mercedes, my dear, I don't know what was written on that slip of paper, but I'll thank you eternally for saying: 'And the winner is Frank Sinatra for *From Here to Eternity.*' . . .

"It's quite a dream. I still have it three nights a week. I'd have it seven nights a week, but I don't go to bed four nights a week.

"Talk about being 'born again.' It's the one time in my life when I had such happiness I couldn't even share it with another human being. I ducked the party, lost the crowds and took a walk. Just me and Oscar. I think I relived my entire lifetime that night as I walked up and down the streets of Beverly Hills. . . .

"Since that night, the roller coaster evened out and every day is the Fourth of July. Yes, I started out the third decade of the Academy of Motion Picture Arts and Sciences as the 'man least likely' and closed it out as a grateful human being, given a second shot at life. . . ."

Altogether, *From Here to Eternity* earned eight Academy Awards, tying *Gone With the Wind* for the most Oscars won, up to that time.

None was more significant than Sinatra's Oscar as Best Supporting Actor.

During the next several years, he was The King again, restored once more to the throne. He did seventeen films in six years; he recorded his best-known, and perhaps his best albums; he virtually named his own price in any night club in the land, and he was on his way to becoming a one-man conglomerate.

He was not an entertainer anymore, nor even a "personality."

He was becoming an empire.

After winning the Oscar, Frank Sinatra reclaimed the entertainment empire that had slipped from him as he turned 35.

He discussed this with Bob Thomas at the time:

"I don't mind the term," he said of the numerous reports of his stunning "comeback."

"It doesn't hurt my feelings and it makes the story sound more dramatic. But I don't think it's true. Maybe I wasn't active in pictures, but I was still making money. I could draw as much salary and in some cases more than I had before in night clubs.

"They used the same term, 'comeback,' with Judy Garland. But she didn't make any comeback. The talent was always there. She just wasn't working."

He said he felt his career troubles had started while he was under contract to MGM, and he was glad he'd got out of it. "I knew I would never get out of sailor suits and Army uniforms unless I left there. So I took my money and got out. They owed me $250,000. I settled for half."

Personal troubles? He admitted they (or was it she?) had had an effect on his career.

"I hear records I made three or four years ago," he said then, "and I wish I could destroy the masters. It was also because of emotion, no doubt about it."

The emotion, of course, was caused by Ava; their stormy courtship was no less stormy after marriage. They were often separated, not only by conflicting careers, but by clashing temperaments as well. Ava was being linked romantically with Spanish bullfighter Luis Miguel Dominguin, with Cuban playboy Porfirio Rubirosa, and with Italian comedian Walter Chiari.

By October, 1953, it had reached the point where she publicly announced, through MGM, that she planned to divorce Sinatra. But it took a while.

Asked about the marriage in 1955, Sinatra reported: "It's at a stalemate. She established

residence in Nevada, but she never filed the papers for divorce. I don't know what she's going to do."

Nevertheless, they attended the premiere of her film, *Mogambo,* together in 1953. The movie—which may have been her best dramatic effort—won her an Academy Award nomination for the role of one of the two women vying for the affections of white hunter Clark Gable. The other woman was Grace Kelly. But the Best Actress Oscar that year was won by Audrey Hepburn for *Roman Holiday.* And on the same night that Frank won his.

After the Awards ceremony, Frank went off to Las Vegas for a personal appearance; Ava went to Palm Springs, then to Italy for *The Barefoot Contessa.*

Newspapers and magazines were linking Frank with Gloria Vanderbilt.

"Sure," he replied. "And what's the penalty for bigamy these days?"

She was still married to Leopold Stokowski, he to Ava.

"I found Gloria delightful company. It was wonderful to hear a woman talk intelligently about music and books. Out here, in Hollywood, the girls seem to limit their conversation to what's happening in Hollywood and at the racetrack."

Miss Vanderbilt was signed to co-star with Frank in *Johnny Concho* in 1956, but was replaced by Phyllis Kirk after a few hours of shooting.

Ava Gardner obtained a Mexican divorce on July 5, 1957, charging Sinatra with desertion.

His problems with, and eventual divorce from Ava were about the only troubles still plaguing Frank as he otherwise prospered during the fifties.

He had made the break with Columbia Records, where one of his last recordings, "Good Night Irene," had sold a mere 150,000 records. He signed with Capitol, and his recording income zoomed to more than a quarter-of-a-million dollars a year. "Songs for Young Lovers," "Swing Easy," and "In the Wee Small Hours" quickly sold 250,000 each.

With Stordahl still as his arranger, Frank cut his first two sides for Capitol in 1953: "I'm Walking Behind You" and "Lean Baby." But these two numbers didn't really make it for

Frank (Eddie Fisher's version of "I'm Walking Behind You" was the big hit).

Then Stordahl left for a television job and was replaced by Nelson Riddle at Capitol. Riddle arranged Frank's next recordings: "I Love You," "South of the Border," "Don't Worry about Me," and "I've Got the World on a String." Then came "My One and Only Love."

"He's stimulating to work with," Riddle said. "You have to be right on mettle all the time. The man himself somehow draws everything out of you. He has the same effect on the boys in the band; they know he means business, so they pull everything out.

"Frank and I both have, I think, the same musical aim. We know what we're each doing with a song, what we want the song to say."

Riddle was to arrange much of Sinatra's movie music as well—and win several Academy Award nominations for his efforts.

Riddle and Sinatra surely were in tune. The new arranger began to alter Frank's moody, lyrical interpretations and, at the same time, added a new jazz beat and a new tempo. His voice took on a more mature appeal; when he sang about love, the sound carried the weight and feeling of experience.

"Learning the Blues" and "Young at Heart" were big hits for Frank then. "Young at Heart"—which eventually hit the million mark—was Number One in 1954, when *Billboard* magazine had him at the top of the vocalist chart, at the top of the disc jockey poll with that song, as well as with the best LP, "Swing Easy."

The development of the eight-song, long-playing record helped Sinatra reach new and bigger listening audiences. "Songs for Swinging Lovers" was named one of the best jazz albums of 1956, and a *Metronome* poll of jazz musicians named him the "musicians' musician" that same year.

"The Bony Baritone" in 1954.

"People often remark that I'm pretty lucky. I don't think luck has much to do with it. You've got to have something more substantial; the competition is too fierce.

"Luck is only important in so far as getting the chance to sell yourself at the right moment. After that, you've got to have talent and learn how to use it."

Frank Sinatra had worked hard to return to the top of the hill and he was right: luck had little to do with it.

The offers came quickly from Hollywood after *From Here to Eternity*. He was scheduled to do *Pink Tights* with Marilyn Monroe, but that fell through because of her script disputes with 20th Century-Fox. He was supposed to co-star with Ava in *St. Louis Woman,* but that project was also dropped.

He signed with United Artists to do a film called *Suddenly,* and it proved beyond question that his *Eternity* performance was no mere one-shot piece of luck. *Suddenly* is a thriller in which Sinatra and Sterling Hayden plot to assassinate the president of the United States (a theme he was to return to later in *The Manchurian Candidate*).

He brought "spine-chilling reality to the role," wrote one critic about Sinatra's performance in *Suddenly.* Another noted that he "holds the screen and commands it with ease, authority, and skill that is, obviously, the result of care, study, work, and an intelligent mind."

Again, in a straight dramatic role, Sinatra confirmed his acting skill.

Frank's hit song, "Young at Heart," was

And with Doris Day in *Young at Heart,* 1953.

44

As the killer in *Suddenly*, 1954. Sinatra advanced his growing reputation as a serious actor (begun in *From Here to Eternity)* with this thriller about a presidential assassination plot.

With Debbie Reynolds in *The Tender Trap*, 1955.

translated into a movie of the same title, a musical remake of *Four Daughters.* He played the down-on-his-luck songwriter originated by John Garfield in the earlier version. Doris Day co-starred with Frank, who sang, along with the title tune, such standards as "Someone to Watch over Me," "Just One of Those Things," "One for My Baby," and "You, My Love."

Not as a Stranger teamed Sinatra with Olivia de Havilland and Robert Mitchum, in this Stanley Kramer production based on Morton Thompson's novel of hospital life and love. No songs in the operating room, and Frank again solidified his acting reputation.

Not as a Stranger was followed by the popular comedy with music, *The Tender Trap,*

Hollywood, November 22, 1955. Arriving at the premiere of *Guys and Dolls* with actress Deborah Kerr.

in which Frank played theatrical agent Charlie Reader, co-starring with Debbie Reynolds, Celeste Holm, and David Wayne.

Once more, reviewers praised his acting talents: "Frank Sinatra shows again that in addition to possessing whatever it is that it takes to be a matinee idol, he also has acting ability."

The opinion of Bosley Crowther, dean of film critics, was telling and significant: "His performance is well-nigh a perfect demonstration of the sort of flippant, frantic thing he can do best. It catches the nervous, restless Frankie at the top of his comedy form. Indeed, it is probably in his timing that his excellence with the quip is achieved, and this leads one to wonder how much his training as a singer contributed to what he is."

Flippant and frantic, nervous and restless, Frank never was one to sit by the telephone.

He was set to play Terry Malloy in *On the Waterfront,* but the role went to Marlon Brando instead. Sinatra was furious with producer Sam Spiegel, felt he had been "screwed," and sued him for half-a-million dollars. That suit wasn't settled until 1960, when Frank had cooled down and agreed to accept far less, a token payment, in fact: a hi-fi stereo system. Marlon Brando popped up again on Sinatra's wrong side when he pitched for the role of the Okinawan interpreter in *Teahouse of the August Moon,* knowing that Brando also wanted the part.

"I think I'm the better type for it," Frank insisted. "Six other guys, including some fine actors, were up for Maggio in *From Here to Eternity,* and I got the part."

But it didn't work for *Teahouse;* Brando got it.

There had been no love lost between the two since they co-starred in *Guys and Dolls,* released in 1955. Brando played Sky Masterson and Frank was Nathan Detroit, proprietor of "the oldest established permanent floating crap game in New York," in this musical version of Damon Runyon's story. Abe Burrows and Jo Swerling had written it for Broadway.

Sinatra's "natural" performing style often clashed with Brando's Actors Studio approach on the set of *Guys and Dolls,* and Frank told director Joe Mankiewicz: "Don't put me in the game, coach, until Mumbles is through rehearsing."

One observer on the set compared the two actors personally: "Sinatra plays God to his entourage; Brando doesn't."

Some felt Brando disliked Sinatra because he felt threatened by him. Though no one any longer disputed Sinatra's acting talent, Brando always referred to him as a "singer."

Guys and Dolls was a hit at the box office, despite less than glorious reviews. Frank sang "The Oldest Established Permanent Floating Crap Game in New York," "Guys and Dolls," "Sue Me," and a solo, "Adelaide," a new tune added to the original Frank Loesser score.

"Sinatra is Sinatra and in this is perfect," wrote one critic.

The role is a "breeze for Frank Sinatra and he plays it as if he were eating a banana split," added Louella Parsons.

But the movie got him into some extracurricular troubles, too.

Columnist Ed Sullivan had a nationwide television variety show, "a really, really big 'shew,' " high on "names" and juggling acts. Sinatra was to appear on the program to plug *Guys and Dolls*. It was a custom of the show to introduce personalities, sometimes from the audience, sometimes on stage, and to "mention" their latest effort. All gratis, of course.

Frank balked at the no-fee appearance, more on principle than anything else, and took the test case to the Screen Actors Guild. Sullivan shot back with a full page ad in *Variety*, noting: "Aside to Frankie Boy: Never mind that tremulous 1947 offer: 'Ed, you can have my last drop of blood.' "

Sinatra answered in kind: "Dear Ed. You are sick.—Frankie. PS—sick, sick, sick."

Of course, fights with the press, in print or in punches, were nothing new to Sinatra, who always felt that reporters invaded his private life. He had made his anger internationally known. His enemies among the press corps included some of the biggest syndicated columnists in the business.

One, a woman—they were particular targets of his wrath—was sitting in the Stork Club one night wearing sunglasses. Sinatra got up from his table and dropped a dollar bill in a coffee cup in front of her.

"I always figured she had to be blind," he said.

He once got into a brawl with *New York Daily Mirror* columnist Lee Mortimer at Ciro's on Hollywood's Sunset Strip. Mortimer had reported what he saw as Frank's connections with the mob, notably with one Lucky Luciano. Mortimer wound up battered and bruised and the case wound up in court. It cost Sinatra dearly, not in dollars—Mortimer settled for an apology and court costs—but in reputation and pride.

Over the years, Frank has had fights with Robert Ruark, Dorothy Kilgallen, Louella Parsons, Hedda Hopper, and Westbrook Pegler. Comic Joey Bishop, a close Sinatra friend, once got a big laugh at a benefit when he followed Sinatra on the show.

One of Frank's earliest run-ins with the press. Columnist Lee Mortimer (L., and glaring), accused Sinatra of striking him at a Hollywood night club. Sinatra appeared in court on April 9, 1947 to answer charges. He pleaded innocent and demanded a jury trial.

"For an encore," said Bishop, "Frank will punch a photographer in the nose."

Sinatra once said: "Why should I give the newspapers anything? I ought to give a cocktail party for the press and put a Mickey Finn in every glass." Another oft-quoted remark: "I hate cops and newspapermen."

He never changed his attitude about the press, although at times he has apologized for his actions and some newspapermen have gotten along quite well with him, indeed consider him a friend. But his outbursts to, and in, the press were not just youthful arrogance or naiveté; his attacks grew tougher as he did, and spread internationally.

He once canceled a Berlin performance after a squabble in the German press. A Mexican newsman accused him of assault and battery in Acapulco in 1971. Washington columnist Maxine Cheshire asked him to apologize publicly for a remark he made at a party in 1973. He once called Chicago columnist Mike Royko a "pimp." In 1970, he sued a *Los Angeles Times* columnist for $2,000,000 and called for a nationwide crusade to rein in the nation's "runaway press."

A friend once tried to analyze Sinatra's constant friction with journalists: "I think he's afraid of the press; he's afraid he'll say the wrong thing. He feels they ask him questions that always get under his skin. He feels his private life is his own and that he has a perfect right off-stage to live it as he wants.

"Basically, of course, he's a really insecure fellow, trying to tell the world he's a great guy. It doesn't show so much now, but once he said, 'Boy, when I come out with "Ol' Man River" and let those deep notes go, I just feel them asking how can a little so-and-so like that do it?'"

"He's a Hoboken kid standing on a corner," said another friend, "daring the gang on the other side of the street to come across. He knows he can't lick them single-handed, but he's going to try anyway. Just to prove something."

Perhaps the most infamous of his rows with the press occurred when he was on tour in Australia in 1974, and he called the journalists waiting to interview him "bums, parasites, hookers, and pimps." He pointed to the women as "the hookers of the press." As a result, Australian labor unions grounded his plane and temporarily refused to work for him.

Columnist Earl Wilson had befriended Sinatra early in the singer's career and for 25 years felt they'd had a close rapport. Then Wilson found himself barred from a Florida opening, and he wrote: "After trying to be an honorable newspaperman with a reputation for getting along with big personalities, to get this slap in the face made me crumble spiritually. The word 'barred' is a degrading one in my business and it had never been used against me before."

For five years Wilson did not talk to, or write about Sinatra, after which he printed some nice things about the singer's 1975 European tour. Then he was invited to the Sinatra–John Denver concert in Nevada and, seemingly, peace was restored.

Wilson ultimately wrote a biography of Sinatra, and was sued for $3,000,000 for writing a book that was "false, fictionalized, boring, and uninteresting." Though the suit conceded that the book was "favorable and complimentary," it also charged that it represented unfair competition to the autobiography that Sinatra intends to write.

In his book, Wilson observed that Sinatra does not like peace in his life, but prefers to be "a warrior, an unhappy warrior. . . . The conflicts make him a bigger box office attraction than all the happy singers. Sinatra knows exactly what he's doing. By protesting that his privacy is being invaded, he gets free advertising for his eccentricities and his bookings. . . .

"In that sense, he had made dupes of the press for thirty to forty years. The press gives him free space to blast the press. It has found no way to refuse him space for his outbursts because he is colorful and controversial, and a story about him may be the most interesting thing in the paper."

And yet . . .

Once a publicity man brought his father to a Sinatra film set. "If I had brought any one of six big-name columnists," the publicist recalled, "Frank would have thrown them off the set. With my father, he couldn't have been more charming. He posed for a picture with him, got all the other stars to pose. Then, later, he saw that all were personally autographed.

"You figure him out."

One of the more frightening directorial figures in film-making is the redoutable Otto Preminger. Frank worked with him on *The Man with the Golden Arm,* the Nelson Algren story of a dope addict.

In the 1950s, this was a hot potato; only a man of Preminger's talent and independence would take it on at the time. He had to persuade the distributors, United Artists, to release it without the Production Code Seal of Approval, the industry's self-censorship precursor of the ratings system.

Sinatra, who seemed to survive, if not thrive, on controversy, took the role of Frankie Machine, an addict who goes "cold turkey" in an effort to withdraw from drugs and straighten out his life. Kim Novak co-starred.

With Kim Novak in *The Man with the Golden Arm,* 1956.

For the key scene, in which Frank has to go through the agonies of withdrawal, Preminger, the perfectionist, scheduled days of rehearsals, takes, and retakes.

Frank reacted with a definite no; he knew at once how he wanted to play the scene.

"Just keep those cameras grinding," he said.

Ultimately, the scene was done with no rehearsal, a brief discussion beforehand, and in one take.

It was a style of acting, and a method of shooting, which earned Frank the very apt nickname, "One-Take Charlie."

"I don't buy this take and retake jazz," he explained. "The key to good acting on the screen is spontaneity and that's something you lose a little with each take."

It was a successful style, at least for *The Man with the Golden Arm*.

Arthur Knight called the performance "truly virtuoso," adding: "The thin, unhandsome, one-time crooner has an incredible instinct for the look, the gesture, the shading of the voice that suggests tenderness, uncertainty, weakness, fatigue, despair. Indeed, he brings to the character much that has not been written into the script, a shade of sweetness, a sense of edgy indestructibility that actually creates the appeal and intrinsic interest of the role."

Sinatra received an Academy Award nomination for the performance, in competition that year with Ernest Borgnine for *Marty*, James Cagney for *Love Me or Leave Me*, James Dean for *East of Eden*, and Spencer Tracy for *Bad Day at Black Rock*—"cherce" company, indeed.

On his arm as he attended the ceremonies at Hollywood's Pantages Theater that night of March 21, 1956, was singer and starlet Peggy Connolly. Some 3,000 spectators outside the theater screamed and shouted for Frank; it was reminiscent of his bobbysox-idol days.

But this time the envelope contained Borgnine's name, not Sinatra's. (It was something of Italian night, however; Anna Magnani won the Best Actress award for *The Rose Tattoo*.)

Working as hard as ever, bounding from screen to stage to studio, Frank had recording sessions that year in February, March, and September.

He worked on the NBC-TV production of "Our Town," a musical version of the Thornton Wilder play, which helped popularize one of Sinatra's biggest hits, "Love and Marriage."

And, on screen, Frank followed *Golden Arm* with an unbilled guest appearance in *Meet Me in Las Vegas*, a musical with Dan Dailey and Cyd Charisse. Sinatra can be spotted around the Sands Hotel—of which he was a part owner.

Despite Sinatra's musical tributes to Chicago, New York, or even foggy London, Las Vegas is really his kind of town. For a guy who sleeps little and hardly knows the meaning of the word 'rest,' a 24-hour town like Vegas — where booze and the company to drink it with are always available—is just the thing.

Las Vegas and Big Money go together. In the fifties, Frank Sinatra had both.

At the end of 1956, he was, for the first time, among the Top Ten Money-Making Stars in the annual *Motion Picture Herald* poll.

Jack Entratter, who once managed the Copacabana in New York, had taken charge of entertainment at that relatively new gambling den in the desert, the Sands Hotel. He wanted Sinatra, who was then appearing at the Flamingo. He invited the singer out to the Sands, offering him the most luxurious accommodations—the three-bedroom Presidential Suite, with a private swimming pool protected by a stone wall.

Frank came, he saw, he conquered. He stayed.

He was treated more than presidentially, he was treated royally. Food, drink, service, for himself, as well as for his guests.

With Frank there, it was a lot easier to lure Dean Martin and Jerry Lewis and, soon after, Sammy Davis Jr. In fact, it was Sinatra who pushed the Davis act; it was then called the Will Mastin Trio, with Sammy as a dancing, drumming dynamo supported by his father and uncle. They became Frank's proteges.

"I love Frank," Sammy was to announce in later years. "He was the kindest man in the world to me when I lost my eye in an auto accident and wanted to kill myself."

Then he added the unkindest cut.

"But there are many things he does that there is no excuse for. I don't care if you are the most talented man in the world, it doesn't give you the right to step on people and treat

At the Sands Hotel, Las Vegas, October 14, 1953.

them rotten. That is what he does occasionally."

Frank took it personally, even though Sammy regretted some of what he said and wanted to apologize. Frank, who had pretty much rewritten a part in *Never So Few* for Sammy, gave it instead to Steve McQueen.

There were also reports of Sammy and Ava together.

Eventually, however, the sores healed and the friendship was renewed. Sammy again became part of the Clan, appearing in the Sinatra-Clan movies: *Ocean's Eleven, Sergeants Three, Robin and the Seven Hoods.*

March 10, 1981. Sinatra and Sammy Davis Jr. (L.) entertaining at a benefit concert in Atlanta, Georgia, to raise funds for the investigation into the multiple murders of black children in that city.

Some members of "The Clan" in 1960. (L. to R.): Peter Lawford, Dean Martin, Sammy Davis Jr., and Sinatra.

Others in the Clan—that Las Vegas clique of Beverly Hills millionaires with Sinatra as their leader—included Peter Lawford, Pat Kennedy Lawford, Milton Berle, Tony Curtis, Janet Leigh, Shirley MacLaine, Dean Martin, Juliet Prowse, Sammy Cahn, Jimmy Van Heusen, Jack Entratter, and Joey Bishop.

With his Las Vegas business interests, as well as an ABC Television deal worth $3,000,000 for 26 half-hour shows and two spectaculars (a deal which lasted a year), the success of Reprise—his own record label—plus other music enterprises, and his own film production company, Sinatra was reported to be making $4,000,000 a year in 1957. Was he?

"I don't know," he told reporters. "All I see is figures on sheets of paper. Last night I couldn't buy the Mike Romanoffs a drink because I had only four dollars in my pocket. Today I asked my business manager for $100 spending money and he turned me down."

Frank did have a sense of humor.

In 1956, through his own film company—with old friend Hank Sanicola as associate producer—Sinatra financed, produced, and starred in *Johnny Concho,* a Western featuring Keenan Wynn and Phyllis Kirk. Originally, Gloria Vanderbilt, with whom Sinatra was having a well-publicized affair, was set for the female lead. The affair over, however, she was replaced by Miss Kirk after one day's shooting.

The Los Angeles Times reviewer, Philip Scheuer, had this comment: "The film apparently represents two wish fulfillments of every Hollywood star—to boss his own company and to play a cowboy. Sinatra has,

With "Clan" members, Dean Martin (L.) and Sammy Davis Jr. (C.), at a SHARE benefit concert in Santa Monica, California. May 21, 1978.

on the whole, done better with the second wish than with the first."

His next film combined nostalgia with pleasure, friendship with business. He played, of all things, a newspaper reporter in *High Society,* the musical remake—with an original score by Cole Porter!—of *The Philadelphia*

Sinatra and Grace Kelly in a scene from *High Society,* 1956.

1955. "Ol' Blue Eyes" as Ol' cowhand, begins work on *Johnny Concho,* his first Western. (Also his first time out as producer.)

Singing with Bing Crosby for an exhibition war bond tournament at the Lakeside Golf Club in Hollywood to promote the sale of a $10,000 bond. (Someone did buy it.) February 1, 1944.

Story, which first starred Cary Grant, Katharine Hepburn, and Jimmy Stewart. In this new version, Sinatra appeared with his early idol, later-to-be friend, Bing Crosby, along with Grace Kelly and Celeste Holm.

"I'm real excited about doing the picture with Bing," he told reporters when he was publicizing *High Society.* "We've been wanting to do one for years. Every time we would see each other, we'd say, 'When are we going to do it?' The answer always was: 'I guess we'll have to wait until the writers come up with a story for us.'

"Leo McCarey almost had one for us. He was going to do a picture with Bob Hope, Bing, and me, but it never panned out."

High Society did pan out. His duet with Bing, "What a Swell Party This Is," is worth the price of admission. Frank also sings "Who Wants to Be a Millionaire?," "Well, Did You Evah?," and "Mind If I Make Love to You?"

He then played the cameo role of a honky-tonk piano player in Mike Todd's *Around the World in 80 Days* before bouncing off to Spain for Stanley Kramer's *The Pride and the Passion,* a $4,000,000 disaster with Cary Grant, Sophia Loren, and a cannon that has to be dragged cross-country for the sake of England's future in the Napoleonic Wars.

Frank brought Peggy Connolly with him on location.

At the same time, Ava announced in Rome that divorce papers had been signed.

While filming outside Madrid, the personality of "One-Take Charlie" took over again. Producer-director Kramer noted that Frank would stay in Madrid, carousing or whatever, until he was needed.

"It used to make me damn mad," Kramer said, "to see him drive up to the set in a taxi at 8 a.m. I was sure he had been up all night watching the gypsies dance flamenco.

"Then he'd take a quick look at the script and say, 'Let's get this circus on the road.' The cameras would turn. One take and I secretly wanted to yell for take after take to make Frank suffer. But I realized he had made the first take come alive—as if he had been rehearsing for a week.

"He is the master of naturalness in acting."

The Joker Is Wild, if it didn't realistically reflect Frank's own career, at least recalled it.

This story, based on the biography of Joe E. Lewis, tells of the famed comedian's start as a cafe singer, his troubles with the mob, his stint in burlesque, before he hits the bottle and the bottom and begins on the long road back. Lewis was a friend of Sinatra's and the parallels are best left to history.

It was a picture Frank wanted to do, having bought the story when it was still in galleys, and he later took a major part in its packaging. He signed Mitzi Gaynor, Jeanne Crain, and Eddie Albert to co-star.

Variety praised Sinatra's work: "He's believable and forceful—alternately sympathetic and pathetic, funny and sad."

Frank sang "I Cried for You," "If I Could Be with You," his well-known "Chicago," and "All the Way," the Van Heusen-Cahn tune which won the Academy Award for Best Song of 1957.

More significantly, *The Joker Is Wild* was one of the films in which Frank had ownership rights or profit participation in addition to his salary.

Columbia studio chief Harry Cohn wanted Frank for the title role in *Pal Joey,* from the Broadway musical by Rodgers and Hart. Cohn originally bought the property for Gene Kelly (who had created the role on the New York

stage), but Kelly apparently asked for too much money.

Cohn negotiated with Frank's MCA agent, Abe Lastfogel. This time, however, unlike *From Here to Eternity,* Sinatra was no longer available for $1,000 a week. Lastfogel outlined the terms: $125,000—plus 25 percent of the profits.

"You're nuts," shouted Cohn.

Lastfogel was firm.

Cohn accepted the terms.

The victory must have held a special pleasure for Sinatra because Marlon Brando also wanted the role.

It had been 17 years since John O'Hara's *Pal Joey* appeared on Broadway, and it worked as well, if not better, on the screen. Frank starred as the classic gilt-edged heel, Joey Evans, with Kim Novak and Rita Hayworth as his playmates. He sings—and sings well— "Bewitched, Bothered and Bewildered" with Rita, "I Could Write a Book," with Kim (whose voice was dubbed by Trudy Erwen), "There's a Small Hotel," "I Didn't Know What Time It Was," and perhaps the most popular, "The Lady Is a Tramp." Nelson Riddle did the musical arrangements.

Sinatra's business negotiations on *The Joker Is Wild* and *Pal Joey* were indicative of his new professional status. He talked about it with Bob Thomas, on the set of *Kings Go Forth* in 1957:

"For the first time in my life, I'm organized. I had to learn the hard way, but now I know that I can only do one thing at a time. Oh, when I think of the energy I wasted ten years ago trying to do everything at once and getting nothing done really well!

"Now I know what I'm doing. All of today, I'll devote my time to this picture, giving it all my concentration. Then I'll go have dinner and go to a recording session from nine to midnight at Capitol Records. In the time I'm going there, I'll adjust my thinking to the making of records."

He admitted psychiatry had a hand in his new philosophy.

"I was under analysis for six months once. The reason was that I had a couple of specific problems I had to work out. I got them off my chest and that was that. I know a lot of people who use psychiatry as a crutch. They can hardly wait to get on that couch and tell something new that has occurred to them. I used it more as a way to talk out my problems. It's the same thing you could do with a close friend.

"But in show business it's hard to have close friends, and I don't feel I should burden them with my problems."

The careful planning was paying off. Sinatra's success was far greater than it had been in his early "swoon-provoking" days, when he took a more scatter-gun approach to his career.

He was able to look down from the top now.

"It's very difficult for me to describe how I feel about it all," he said. "I'm older now and I have a better appreciation of the realities. I like to have fun, but I find I'm spending more time with the children and enjoying it.

"I used to think it was important to have a lot of clothes. Now there's twelve suits instead of thirty suits in the closet, six pairs of shoes instead of twenty-five, and, like most guys, I buy about six new ties a year.

"I'm just as happy."

Humphrey Bogart died on January 14, 1957, after a long illness.

Frank and Bogie had been close friends since the Holmby Hills days, when they were neighbors and "officers" of the Rat Pack. Both had liked to work hard and play hard, although Bogie preferred to play at home. Frank was a high liver; Bogie played it pretty close to the vest. Bogie liked to sail on his yacht Santana; Frank's idea of sailing was to rent a power boat, completely furnished with band, booze, and broads.

Yet, few men were closer. Once, when Bogart left the hospital after he'd been diagnosed as having cancer, Frank gave him his Palm Springs house to use as he wished. When Bogie returned home, Frank was a nightly visitor whenever he was in town.

When Bogart died, Sinatra was working at the Copacabana in New York. He was so upset, he knew he couldn't perform. "I can't go on," he phoned the Copa management. "I'm afraid I wouldn't be coherent."

Sammy Davis Jr. and Jerry Lewis filled in for him.

In the weeks after the funeral, Sinatra, along with the David Nivens, the Mike Romanoffs, and others, dropped in to cheer up Betty Bacall.

During her period of mourning, Betty rarely went out. If she went out at all, it was most often with Frank. He had been a good friend for years and his carefree, high-living ways seemed to be the best medicine for her at this time. They went to an Adlai Stevenson political rally together, and then attended a closed-circuit television showing of the middleweight championship fight.

Frank asked her to accompany him and a planeload of friends to Las Vegas for the premiere of The Joker Is Wild. As part-owner of the Sands Hotel, he took over the cocktail lounge after the opening for an Italian breakfast, which didn't break up until after six in the morning. Betty sat at Frank's right. At all his small dinner parties, she was the hostess.

The couple was reported to be romantically involved. These rumors were stoked by columnists who noted that Frank had just bought the late Al Jolson's estate in Palm Springs for $90,000 and that the three-bedroom house with two poolside guest cottages might be just right for Betty Bacall and her two children. Then Frank added a swimming pool to his Beverly Hills hilltop house, though he never went in much for swimming. Betty's youngsters did, however.

In March, 1958, Hollywood columnist Louella Parsons reported that Sinatra and Bacall would marry.

But once the story got into the press, Sinatra left Hollywood and Betty became unavailable for comment. A few weeks later, she departed for London to film Flame over India, to be shot in India, Spain, and England.

In her autobiography, Lauren Bacall says she did have an affair with Frank Sinatra and that it was his decision not to get married; she was most interested.

She writes that at one point Frank did propose to her, and she was "giddy with joy" at the prospect. "My face radiated happiness. I said nothing to anyone, but now I knew my life would go on, the children would have a father, I would have a husband, we'd have a home again."

As leader of the Spanish guerrillas in *The Pride and the Passion*.

The Pride and the Passion, 1956. A Stanley Kramer film about Spanish guerrilla warfare against Napoleon's French troops. (L. to R.): Sophia Loren, Sinatra, Cary Grant.

"Ol' Blue Eyes" in 1951.

June 16, 1979. In a nostalgic look back 40 years, Sinatra and Harry James perform their old arrangement of "All or Nothing at All" in Los Angeles.

But when the news got out, Frank called her—to say goodbye. It was the end of what she called "our exciting, imperfect, not-to-be-love-affair."

Eventually, the two became good friends again, something that was true of nearly all Frank's ladies, wives included.

"I'll always have a special feeling for him," Bacall wrote. "The good times we had were awfully good."

Sinatra in the fifties seemed to be king of all he surveyed. And he surveyed a great deal: movies; night clubs (especially those with gambling interests); records; various commercial investments, including real estate.

Yet, there were some areas of contention as well; his volatile (Sicilian?) personality seemed unable to avoid them for long.

He got into a contract dispute with 20th Century-Fox over his role in the Rodgers and Hammerstein musical *Carousel*. He walked off the Maine location site and Fox brought a $1,000,000 breach of contract suit against him, and hired Gordon MacRae to take over the role of Billy Bigelow. Ironically, the point of contention—dual shooting in both Cinemascope and Todd-AO versions—was ultimately meaningless, since the film was finally shot in the 55mm process only. But without Frank Sinatra. The breach of contract suit was later dropped.

One courtroom adventure had some comic overtones, though probably not for Frank. It became known as "The Case of the Wrong Door Raid," and involved another Italian of note, Joe DiMaggio, the Yankee Clipper. Back in 1954, DiMaggio had been left by his wife Marilyn Monroe and was in a state over it. A private detective had told Joe that Marilyn was having an affair—with another woman.

Frank, in his best *padrone* style, offered to help his friend. Two private detectives were hired and a posse of *paisanos* broke into the woman's apartment. But, wrong door. The very surprised, innocent woman sued for $200,000 worth of damages in a well-publicized case which came up in 1957.

Sinatra and DiMaggio were cleared by a grand jury, which accepted testimony that they had remained outside during the raid. The suit was ultimately settled out of court for an undisclosed sum.

In the same year, Sinatra sued *Look* magazine for $2,300,000, charging libel in a three-part profile published that May. He later switched the charge to invasion of privacy, then dropped it altogether.

More significantly, his television series for

On location in Paris for *Kings Go Forth,* 1957. Sinatra plays a WWII amputee infantry lieutenant.

ABC, despite the inclusion of an hour-long special with Bing Crosby, was disappointing and was dropped after one season. Television (with the exception of an NBC production of *Our Town* with Eva Marie Saint and Paul Newman) seemed the one medium Sinatra couldn't conquer.

His film *Kings Go Forth,* a World War II "romantic drama" with Tony Curtis and Natalie Wood, got a cool reception.

And there were location problems in the filming of *Some Came Running,* shot partly in Madison, Indiana—not Frank's kind of town. But, then, Frank's carousing with co-star Dean Martin was not exactly accepted behavior in that small Midwestern community. There were disputes with director Vincente Minnelli, too.

About the only bright spot in the *Some Came Running* venture was Shirley MacLaine. "The surprise hit," beamed one critic, "is Shirley MacLaine's touching, unforgettable portrait of the crude, pathetic little floozy who falls in love with Frank." It earned her an Academy Award nomination as Best Actress, though the Oscar that year went to Susan Hayward for *I Want to Live.*

Yet, Sinatra's singing during this period was as good as ever, and the sale of his records was evidence enough that he was still The King. *Down Beat* named him top male vocalist of 1957-58 as did *Metronome,* which noted: "Sinatra devoured this one; there was no chance for anyone else."

His best-selling albums were "Come Fly with Me," "Where Are You?," and "Sinatra's Christmas Album." "Come Fly with Me"—the best-selling album of 1958—was recorded with Billy May as arranger.

May's style was very different from Nelson Riddle's. "Nelson will come to the session with all the arrangements carefully and neatly worked out beforehand," Sinatra said. "But with Billy, you sometimes don't get the copies of the next number until you've finished the last one; he'd still be scribbling away right up to the start of the session."

Frank also worked with Gordon Jenkins, a more relaxed arranger. The "No One Cares" album he did with Jenkins was his last studio session for Capitol Records. Frank's contract with them gave his own recording company the copyright on his master tapes, and he was anxious to do things his way. Capitol reminded him that their deal didn't run out until 1962, but Frank just stopped recording in May 1959 to form Reprise Records.

The corporate Sinatra owned Essex Films and its subsidiaries; four music publishing companies; hotel and gambling interests in Las Vegas and Lake Tahoe, Nevada; radio station partnerships with Danny Kaye; and various real estate enterprises.

Rest? Never heard of it.

"I don't mind work," he said in an understatement. "I had two weeks off after *Golden Arm* and went down to my house in Palm Springs. After two days, I was refreshed. After eleven days, I was clamoring to get back to work. I want to keep busy. The only thing I want to avoid is getting too tied up, so I can't break away to do an exciting picture that might come up in a hurry."

One of the properties that Frank found exciting was Arnold Schulman's brawling comedy, *A Hole in the Head,* which he bought for his own production company. He wanted Frank Capra to direct it. Capra is perhaps the finest director of film comedy in the history of the medium, with such films as *It Happened One Night* and *Arsenic and Old Lace* to his credit.

According to Capra, the offer was a package deal arranged through MCA for Sinatra, Capra, and Schulman—all MCA clients. Sinatra also wanted Edward G. Robinson to play the part of the square brother. The offer to Capra was for one-third ownership of the film; Frank would have the rest.

"Does Sinatra know I make my own films, make all the decisions?" asked Capra.

"He knows. 'Get me Capra,' he said."

Capra recalls the meeting with Frank, some 15 years after he had gone with Jimmy Durante to hear the young singer at the Copa.

"He was a few pounds heavier and many hairs lighter than the Copa Frankie," Capra writes in his autobiography. "But much, much more charming—no. The word is fascinating. No. He's more than that. Fact is, it's difficult to describe a once-in-a-lifetime star. That's what Frank Sinatra was, and still is—a superstar. Brighter than he's ever shone. Bigger than he thinks he is—and it scares him; makes him mean at times.

A moment of fun during the shooting of *Never So Few,* 1957. Frank helps celebrate the July 4th birthday of his co-star, Gina Lollobrigida.

"Champagne explodes when you bottle it in a beer bottle."

As Capra tells it, the meeting was short and sweet.

Frank: "Why don't you and I make *Hole in the Head* together? You do all the dirty work, while I smile and knock off all the broads . . . "

The deal was on.

Capra offers an incisive analysis of Frank's talents:

"Sinatra is a great singer ('a saloon singer' he calls himself) and he knows it. The excitement of moving and reaching the hearts of live audiences with his lyrical virtuosity makes his blood run hot. He has total command of his performances; selects his own songs, songwriters, orchestras, audiences.

"Sinatra is also a great actor, and he knows that, too. But in films he is not Sinatra doing Sinatra's thing with song. He cannot reach and bewitch live, ever-changing 'saloon'

audiences. He performs for a never-changing audience of busy, dispassionate cameramen, sound men, script girls, make-up people, dead-pan electricians who have 'seen it all before,' and other actors who don't bewitch easily—if at all.

"Nor is Sinatra in total command of the shooting of the film. There are budgets and schedules to confine and directors to heed. But Sinatra 'heeds' very badly.

"If directors keep him busy, he maintains an easy truce, for having started something, Sinatra's next goal is to finish it—but fast. He bores easily; can't sit still or be alone; must be where the action is—preferably with his 'saloon' performers, the lovelies, or the less orthodox socially.

"Should he not be used for a day or two—especially on location—Frank grouses, accuses the director of fooling around with the inconsequentials. Regrettably, he is half-right. 'I'm giving you until tomorrow night to shoot my scenes.' And directors do finish with him when he demands—admitting Sinatra is half-right."

In one scene in *Hole in the Head,* Sinatra, Robinson, and Keenan Wynn are working together. In the first rehearsal, Sinatra is great, but the others need more work. During the second rehearsal, Sinatra starts to cool off, as the others get better. By the first camera take, Sinatra is cool and the others are fine.

So, the wily Capra makes a private deal with Keenan Wynn to change cues, mix up the lines, anything to make Sinatra work spontaneously.

"Sinatra had the first line. Keenan jumps him with, 'What'd you say?'

" 'I ain't said nothing yet.'

" 'Well, say it. What's on your mind?'

"It was a brand new game. They play a wonderful scene, full of natural ad libs."

The film worked well and included a bonus: the Van Heusen-Cahn song, "High Hopes," won the Academy Award for Best Song of 1959.

Sinatra finished out the decade with *Never So Few* and *Can-Can.*

Never So Few co-starred Gina Lollobrigida, Peter Lawford, and Steve McQueen—the latter a replacement for Sammy Davis Jr., with whom Sinatra was feuding at the

Down to business. Frank and Gina back to work on
Never So Few.

With Juliet Prowse in Hollywood, May 13, 1960.

As a convict in *The Devil at 4 O'Clock,* 1961.

time—in a World War II drama set in Burma and China. It proved to be a good vehicle for McQueen, who was most impressive.

Can-Can co-starred Sinatra with Shirley MacLaine, Maurice Chevalier, Louis Jourdan, and a young South African dancer named Juliet Prowse. It featured the Cole Porter songs, "I Love Paris," "C'est Magnifique," "Let's Do It," and "It's All Right with Me."

It was shot on the Fox lot during a visit to the United States by Soviet Premier Nikita Khrushchev, who had toured Disneyland as well. The Communist leader gave the film some pre-release press with his assessment that the can-can was "immoral."

It was also the beginning of Sinatra's romance with Juliet Prowse. He eventually proposed to the leggy beauty, an engagement which lasted forty-four days, before it was called off in a terse announcement from each of their public relations spokesmen. "Conflict of career interests" was the official reason given.

A Sinatra friend said: "Frank wants a full-time wife, not one he will have to share with the American public. He did that once with Ava. That was the blackest period of his life.

"Ava's career was going full blast while Frank was on the skids. He followed her all through Europe and to Africa while she made *Mogambo.* He had been a big star and now he was a movie star's husband. It hurt Frank's pride and that's something he's got a lot of. Frank isn't going to hit the skids again, so

there's no danger of Juliet's career outshining his. But he still wants to be the boss if he's going to get married."

And a friend of Miss Prowse's said: "Juliet is 25 and immensely talented. She hasn't yet reached her potential in show business and that's something she's worked for all her life. Supposing she did quit her career. What's she supposed to do all day?

"This is still a strange country to her; she has few friends. You know Frank wouldn't spend all his time with her. He'd be working on pictures, or night clubs, or TV, or he'd be in business conferences. What kind of life would she have?"

Others pointed out still another difference: 21 years.

Sinatra was 45 in 1960. But there was no let-up in his work schedule; if anything, he was putting in longer days (and nights, if that were possible).

He produced, but did not appear in, *X-15* for United Artists, and he co-starred with Spencer Tracy in *The Devil at Four O'Clock,* filmed partly in Hawaii. Tracy had a post-production compliment to pay Sinatra, the actor: "Don't get overconfident around him in a scene."

Frank joined Bing Crosby and Bob Hope on the road, playing a spaceman along with Dean Martin in a guest appearance in *The Road to Hong Kong.*

Frank Sinatra in 1963.

The barber is Anita Ekberg; the film, *Four for Texas;* the year, 1963.

And, while Frank was appearing in Las Vegas, he and his Clan buddies decided to put their camaraderie on film, coming up with some basically flimsy but entertaining plots. The quartet of Clan movies, either personally produced or wholly financed by Sinatra, included *Ocean's Eleven,* with Sinatra, Dean Martin, Sammy Davis Jr., Peter Lawford, Angie Dickinson, Richard Conte, and Joey Bishop; *Sergeants Three,* a U.S. Cavalry update of *Gunga Din,* with Sinatra, Martin, Lawford, and Davis; *Four for Texas,* a Western Clanbake with Martin, Anita Ekberg, and Ursula Andress; and *Robin and the Seven Hoods* (Robin Hood in 1920s Chicago, it featured the Van Heusen-Cahn songs "My Kind of Town," "Style," "Don't Be a Do-Badder," and "Mr. Booze."

Ocean's Eleven, which involved a plot to rip off five Vegas hotels on New Year's Eve, was the first (1960), and the most successful. While shooting it, Frank spent part of his afternoons also filming a cameo role in *Pepe,* rehearsed in the evening for a television show, and at night appeared on stage at the Sands.

But Sinatra began to face some real problems as he became actively involved in politics at the beginning of the sixties, problems partly caused by his Clan connections, partly by certain other "connections."

Politics, of course, was no strange bedfellow to Frank. His mother Dolly was a well-known local Democrat in Hoboken when Frank was growing up. Possibly he was aware, even at that early age, of the influence politics could have on his life.

How much Dolly's political friendships had to do with Frank's early career is still open to question.

It is clear, however, that in 1943, just before his record-breaking third appearance at the Paramount Theater in New York, Sinatra was invited to the White House to meet President Franklin D. Roosevelt. This was the man his son was named after—Franklin Wayne Sinatra Jr.

Toots Shor, owner of New York's Toots Shor Restaurant in midtown Manhattan, and Rags Ragland, a burlesque and night club comedian, were invited along with Frank. Actually, it was Toots who was invited, through a regular restaurant customer, Democratic National Chairman Robert Hannegan. Two dozen or so others were also asked to "tea." All had to be approved by FDR's secretary, Marvin McIntyre.

The president knew of Sinatra, of course, and when Frank was presented to him, he turned to McIntyre and remarked: "Mac, imagine this guy making them swoon. He would never have made them swoon in our day, right?"

He asked Frank the same question: how did he do it, did he know how he had "revived the charming art of fainting" among women?

"No, I wish to hell I did know," Sinatra replied.

Soon after this visit, Sinatra donated $7,500 to the Democratic Party, at a time when he could little afford it.

In 1946, after FDR's death, Sinatra attended the dedication of the Roosevelt home in Hyde Park, New York, as a national shrine. The bobbysoxers almost destroyed the solemnity of that occasion with their shrieks and moans.

Later, Frank also supported Adlai Stevenson, lending his name and presence (along with those of other entertainment personalities, including Lauren Bacall) to Stevenson's unsuccessful bid for the White House.

By 1958, Sinatra was solidly behind the candidacy of John F. Kennedy, then senator from Massachusetts. This was partly due to Frank's connection with Peter Lawford, a fellow Clan member who was also married to Kennedy's sister, Pat.

Through 1958 and 1959, Sinatra gave his name, his reputation, his time, and his influence to support Kennedy for the presidency. By election time, the joke was that if Kennedy were elected, Sinatra would be ambassador to Italy. And Dean Martin Secretary of the Liquor Cabinet.

With the help of Sinatra-produced Kennedy rallies, which included the support of Judy Garland, Sammy Davis Jr., Milton Berle, George Jessel, Mort Sahl, Joe E. Lewis, Ella Fitzgerald, Gene Kelly, Ethel Merman, Leonard Bernstein, Alan King, Nat "King" Cole, Bette Davis, Harry Belafonte, Sidney Poitier, even Eleanor Roosevelt, there was, in the end, a President John F. Kennedy.

With Mrs. Eleanor Roosevelt prior to her appearance on Sinatra's ABC television show. February, 1960.

January 19, 1961. Sinatra escorts Mrs. John Kennedy into the National Guard Armory for the President's Inaugural Gala.

At a pre-Inaugural gala, President Kennedy said: "We are all indebted to a great friend, Frank Sinatra. Tonight we saw excellence."

After the Presidential Inauguration and Ball, Kennedy found time to make an appearance at Sinatra's private party at the Statler Hilton in New York. The next morning, Frank had breakfast with Bobby Kennedy, the president's brother and new attorney-general, and the Peter Lawfords.

A plaque on a bedroom door of Sinatra's Palm Springs house read: "John F. Kennedy Slept Here November 6th and 7th, 1960."

But on another visit soon after, President Kennedy stayed as a house guest with Bing Crosby at Palm Desert instead of with Sinatra as originally planned. This was at the insistence of Bobby Kennedy and other close JFK aides,

who felt Sinatra's friends were too closely related to organized crime.

Sinatra had been regarded as a problem in that respect for some time. Bobby Kennedy worried about Frank's "friendships" with recognized crime leaders like Sam "Momo" Giancana. He had the FBI reopen files on earlier investigations linking Sinatra to Willie Moretti in Jersey City and Lucky Luciano in Havana.

Pete Hamill once wrote that "the mob runs through [Frank's] story like an underground river. He is the most investigated American performer since John Wilkes Booth, and although he has never been indicted or convicted of any mob-related crime, the connection is part of the legend."

On September 11, 1963, *The Associated*

Press transmitted this story:

BULLETIN

Carson City, Nev. (AP)—
The Nevada Gaming Control
Board today issued a complaint
against Frank Sinatra, charging
the singer with playing host to a
notorious Chicago underworld
figure at his Lake Tahoe resort,
the Cal-Neva Lodge.

The complaint alleges the
crooner knowingly hosted
Momo Salvatore (Sam)
Giancana at the lodge between
July 17 and July 28.

Giancana was described in
the Gaming Board complaint as
"one of the twelve overlords in
the . . . Mafia."

The complaint went on: "Frank Sinatra
has for a number of years past maintained and
continued social associations with said Sam
Giancana while knowing his unsavory and
notorious reputation and has openly stated that
he intends to continue such association in
defiance [of Nevada gaming law]."

The Board said Sinatra had ignored a
Nevada-issued "black book" list of eleven
persons unwelcome at gaming establishments.

Sinatra was given two weeks to reply to
the complaint. Instead, he withdrew his license
and sold his holdings in the Cal-Neva and
Sands casinos—worth more than
$3,000,000—but held on to the hotel interest.

A Reno newspaper, the *Nevada State
Journal-Reno Gazette,* in 1980 printed a
posthumous interview with Ed Olsen, the
Gaming Control Board official who pressed the
complaint. The report said President Kennedy
had tried unsuccessfully to influence the 1963
investigation in Sinatra's favor.

In the interview, done for the University of
Nevada's Oral History Department in 1967,
Olsen said the President told then-Governor
Sawyer, "Aren't you people being a little hard
on Frank out here?"

Sinatra wasn't to win back his Nevada
license until 1981. And then he got it with the
help of a state report clearing him of the
persistent rumors about his ties to organized
crime.

The State Gaming Commission praised
Sinatra for his charitable works, chastised the
news media for reporting what the Commission
claimed were unfounded rumors of organized
crime connections, and voted four-to-one to
grant Sinatra a "key employees" license.

One character witness for Sinatra was
President Ronald Reagan.

But back in the fall of 1963, the world was
shocked by more stunning news. The
assassination of President John F. Kennedy in
Dallas on November 22 left Sinatra devastated,
as it did so many others.

"I don't believe it," Sinatra said, shaking
his head as he was told the news while on a
film location. "I really don't believe it. It's a
great loss to the world."

Ironically, this happened only a year after
the release of *The Manchurian Candidate,* a
Sinatra movie dealing with a presidential
assassination plot.

At about the same time *The Manchurian
Candidate* was getting fine reviews, a skinny
18-year-old singer was making his debut at
Disneyland.

Taking the microphone in both hands, the
frail-looking youngster leaned backward, closed
his eyes, and in a mellow baritone sang: "Night
and day, You are the one . . ."

And, "All of me . . . Why not take
awwwwwl of me . . . ."

The resemblance was uncanny.

It was, of course, Frank Sinatra Jr., and he
seemed to be re-creating the animal charm of
his father that, 20 years earlier, had brought the
bobbysoxers to states of ecstasy.

Frank Jr. was a music major at the
University of Southern California when he
decided to go the singing route on his own.
During summer vacations, he had worked as a
bank teller, a film projectionist, and a camp
counselor; his mother insisted he work every
summer to learn self-sufficiency.

When he visited Disneyland that summer
of 1962, he asked the Elliot Brothers if he
could sing with their band—much the same
way his father had started out. "I didn't tell the
band leader who I was," Frank Jr. was to recall
later. "He asked me, 'What makes you think
you can sing?' I told him I wouldn't be asking if
I thought I'd make a fool of myself."

Frank Jr. was given a chance and the

orchestra leader was impressed. His identity wasn't revealed until the bass player—who had once been with the Tommy Dorsey band (where Sinatra Sr. got his start)—recognized him.

After Disneyland, young Frank began making television appearances, including one with Jack Benny, an old family friend; this was the young man's first appearance on a coast-to-coast network broadcast.

He didn't know his father had cut short his own recording rehearsal to watch the program. Frank Sr. laughed with pleasure through the whole show and kept saying, "The kid is really good!"

When a press agent told Frank Sr. that his son was anxious to know what his father thought of the performance, the older Sinatra said: "He can wait; he's a little young."

Ironically, after several TV appearances, young Frank got a job offer from the Tommy Dorsey band, then conducted by Sammy Donahue. The career similarities continued.

Although they hadn't lived together since Frank Jr. was four years old, father and son had always been close. Whatever else, Frank Sr. got high marks for his relations with his children. Frank Jr. idolized his father.

"I've studied with Frank Sinatra, although he doesn't know I've studied with him," he once said. "But I've been following him around all my life and I've heard him everywhere. I've been hanging around movie sets and recording studios since I can remember.

"I've got to prove myself. And that isn't going to be easy. People are not going to compare me with the average entertainer. They're going to compare me with my father—and he's an absolute phenomenon."

Young Frank's notices were good, too; perhaps too good.

He had played such spots as the Flamingo in Las Vegas, the Americana Hotel in New York, the Coconut Grove in Los Angeles, and a return engagement at Disneyland. He was touring with the Tommy Dorsey band when it happened . . .

Young Frank was kidnapped from his motel room at Lake Tahoe, just before he was to go on stage.

John Foss, a trumpet player who was in the room with him at the time, said two

With Frank Jr., December, 1962.

With Frank Jr. at the Americana Hotel in New York, September, 1963. The younger Sinatra was headlining the show at the Royal Box.

gunmen burst in, pretending to be room service. One of them asked, "Where's the money?" and made his captors lie on the floor. Then he tied them up and ordered Sinatra (clad only in his shorts) to put on his trousers. A coat was thrown around the young singer, as the two gunmen dragged him from the room.

Sinatra Sr. was about to start filming *Robin and the Seven Hoods* at Warner Bros. studios when he got the news. He raced to his chartered two-engine plane and flew to the scene of the abduction.

For two days, the FBI, along with California and Nevada lawmen, combed the rugged High Sierras for clues. At one point, an FBI source was quoted as saying, "The kid's life is at stake."

Sinatra Sr. stayed by the telephone at a Reno hotel throughout the ordeal, flying off only for a few hours to visit Nancy and their two daughters, or to confer with FBI agents. Calls and telegrams poured in from all over the world. Attorney General Bobby Kennedy called to assure Sinatra that all the resources of the Justice Department were being deployed. Other calls came: from Pierre Salinger, White House press secretary; from California Governor Jerry Brown. Garry Moore offered the use of his radio program to broadcast a plea to the kidnappers.

Sinatra jumped every time the phone rang. Usually, though, it was a sympathetic friend or a curious caller, and these calls were quickly switched to another telephone so the line could be kept open.

A bowl of soup was all he had to eat during the first 30 hours of waiting.

"I just don't understand it," he said. "I can't figure why."

Then, in the early hours of December 12, 1963—Frank Sr.'s forty-sixth birthday—the kidnappers turned the young man loose on a freeway two miles from his mother's Bel-Air home.

Sinatra told newsmen he had paid $240,000 ransom to get the boy back; no questions asked. Young Frank was not hurt, but, he said, "I was scared."

The kidnappers were later caught and almost all the money was recovered. In March, 1964, three men were found guilty of kidnapping and sentenced to lengthy jail terms.

Frank Jr. continued his singing career and, in 1966, made his movie debut in *A Man Called Adam.*

Meanwhile, daughter Nancy was pursuing

Following his safe release from kidnappers, Frank Jr. is the center of attention with sister Tina (L.) and mother Nancy (R.). December 11, 1963.

The two Franks in 1966.

a show business career of her own. As a child, she had been "immortalized" with her father's song, "Nancy with the Laughing Face." She had attended the University of Los Angeles High School and had spent one semester at the University of Southern California. She worked as a secretary for a while, but left to study drama in New York, thinking always of a show business career.

Nancy appeared in a TV special welcoming Elvis Presley back from his Army stint, after which, in Las Vegas in 1965, she married singer Tommy Sands. She cut some records for Reprise, her father's company, but didn't have much success with them. Then, after her divorce from Sands, she joined up with independent record producer Lee Hazlewood, who was also a songwriter and singer.

Their first recording was "So Long, Babe," followed by "These Boots Are Made for Walking." "Boots" quickly made it to the top and Nancy's career shot up. "After recording so many records with so little success," she said about her new popularity: "it's pretty hard to believe what's happening."

She noted that her father was pleased, too. "Now he calls me 'star.' "

After that, hit records were not uncommon, nor were movie offers. Her films include *For Those Who Think Young, Wild Angels,* and *Speedway,* and she appeared with her father in a small role in *Marriage on the Rocks.* She also recorded the popular theme song from the movie *You Only Live Twice* in 1967, as well as a single with Sinatra Sr., "Somethin' Stupid."

She married television director Hugh Lambert in Cathedral City, California, on December 12, 1970. It was her father's 55th birthday.

"Daddy likes to give things away on his birthday," she said.

The couple presented him with his first grandchild, a girl, in 1974.

The youngest Sinatra daughter, Tina, also grabbed for the show business ring. She started

Performing with daughter Nancy on "A Man and His Music-Part II," December 7, 1966.

in 1968 as a member of a film crew touring Europe making television travelogues and documentaries. She acted in a few television plays, but, in the end, seemed less interested in a show business career than her older brother and sister.

Early in 1981, the 32-year-old Tina, divorced from Wes Farrell, married businessman Richard Cohen at her mother's house in Beverly Hills.

There were few things left untried—and unconquered—for Frank Sinatra as he neared his fiftieth birthday.

Since 1961, he had been an independent recording star, free of his contract with Capitol, and recording exclusively through his own company, Reprise. In that year, he managed 17 recording sessions, producing nearly 70 songs. Among his output were three albums: "Ring-a-Ding-Ding," from one of his more popular expressions; "Swing Along with Me;" and the nostalgic "I Remember Tommy," a tribute to Tommy Dorsey.

Nelson Riddle's contract with Capitol expired in 1963, and he collaborated with Frank on "The Concert Sinatra" and "Sinatra's Sinatra." A deal with Count Basie and his arranger, Neil Hefti, resulted in the album "Sinatra-Basie," a best-seller in 1963. That was also the year Bing Crosby signed up with Reprise, telling newsmen: "Let's face it— Sinatra is a king. He is a very sharp operator, a keen record chief, and has a keen appreciation of what the public wants."

Frank's younger daughter Tina (L.) weds record company executive, Wes Farrell (far L.) at Caesar's Palace, January 27, 1974. With Sinatra is his daughter Nancy.

Sinatra in an NBC, hour-long TV color special, "A Man and His Music," November 24, 1965, featuring 25 years of his hit songs.

(L. to R.): Sinatra, Bing Crosby, Sammy Davis Jr., and Dean Martin during a recording session at Frank's Reprise Record Co., in California. 1965.

Crosby once paid Frank the ultimate compliment:

"I'm a crooner," Bing said. "Frank is a singer and a much better one than I. He's certainly the greatest of our time and probably the greatest entertainer, too."

Then he added:

"He's the type of singer who comes along once in a lifetime. But why did he have to come in my lifetime?"

Reprise was doing well enough that Jack Warner, of Warner Bros., wanted to buy the company. When Frank was named "assistant to the president" at Warners in 1963, he sold Reprise to Jack Warner for $10,000,000 in a three-part deal which was concluded in 1969.

As for films, after *The Manchurian Candidate*, Sinatra did the movie version of the

Neil Simon play, *Come Blow Your Horn,* with Lee J. Cobb, Molly Picon, and Jill St. John. Then a cameo role—in disguise—as the gypsy stableman in *The List of Adrian Messenger.*

What was left for him? Directing?

His one and only try at film directing was *None But the Brave,* a war movie set on a small Pacific island. But, suggested some, hadn't he always been a director, even when he was "just" an actor?

One director who had worked with Sinatra on several pictures said: "I must confess that Frank never ordered, demanded, or even pleaded on how a scene should be shot. But he often suggested.

"A Sinatra suggestion is more than a suggestion. It's an implied command."

Nonetheless, with his own company,

Artanis (Sinatra spelled backwards), Frank directed *None But the Brave,* also appearing in the film, along with Clint Walker, son-in-law Tommy Sands, and Brad Dexter.

"The toughest thing I had to do on the first day of shooting," Sinatra admitted, "was to say 'print.' It took me ten minutes, because I liked the take, but I figured the minute I say 'print,' I'm on the record, the race is off, it's gone, the horses are running around."

Sinatra the director was as much the perfectionist as Sinatra the recording star, but quite the opposite of Sinatra the actor—the one-take specialist.

A young actor, hired for a bit part that took less than ten seconds on the screen, spoke his one line and made a fast exit, when he heard the director calling after him.

"Hey, Charlie."

(Sinatra called everybody Charlie, including girls.)

"You make an exit like that and you walk right out of the picture business. There's nothing more important in show business than getting off the stage."

Then, for 15 minutes, he patiently taught the young actor how to exit at the right camera angle.

"I first felt the urge to direct five years ago," said Sinatra. "Directing is the real challenge in this business. Movies are a director's medium."

Then Sinatra the actor stepped in front of the cameras and did a scene in which he amputates the leg of a wounded Japanese soldier. The act of mercy produces a temporary truce between the Marines and the Japanese soldiers.

Sinatra the actor did the scene in one take.

Sinatra the director yelled, "Print it."

Parts of *None But the Brave* were shot on location off the coast of Hawaii. At one point during filming there, a Hawaiian radio station reported that Sinatra had drowned. Indeed, he had come close.

Sinatra and Ruth Koch, wife of executive producer Howard Koch, were swimming off the island of Kauai, despite a strong undertow. Suddenly they were being sucked into the ocean. It was only the quick action of actor Brad Dexter—who, along with a surfboard crew, swam quickly out to rescue the pair— that saved their lives.

Von Ryan's Express, 1964. Disguised as an SS officer, Sinatra, playing Colonel Joe Ryan, manages to seize a train loaded with 1,000 prisoners and reroute it to Switzerland, instead of Germany.

Brad Dexter would never again want for work.

Frank's next film project was *Von Ryan's Express,* for producer Saul David. David recalls that adventure in his autobiography, *The Industry—Life in the Hollywood Fast Lane.*

Fox had *Von Ryan's Express,* a novel by David Westheimer, adapted for the screen by Wendell Mayes and Joseph Landon. Darryl Zanuck, head of Fox studios, worked out a deal with Sinatra. David recalls that beginning:

"I didn't really think of Sinatra as an actor—his adventures were in a part of the newspaper I didn't read. *Man with a Golden Arm? From Here to Eternity?* Sure. But *Robin and the Seven Hoods? Ocean's Eleven? Sergeants Three?*

"Everybody says he's nothing but trouble."

David reports that he was told, "Sure, but he's going to be your star, so 'you better figure out how to love him.'

With co-star Trevor Howard in *Von Ryan's Express*. Howard, who plays a British major, is also disguised as an SS officer.

Sinatra and Howard during a break in the shooting of *Von Ryan's Express*.

"Dick Zanuck, [Darryl's son] told me Sinatra had called and announced he was going to play Ryan.

" 'What do you mean, "announced"?'

" 'Wait', said Dick, 'You'll see.'

"It was something like a treaty. There were lawyers and helpers, spokesmen on mysterious errands, which probably involved the location of [Sinatra's] parking spaces, offices—who knows?

"The man himself was at Warner Bros., finishing up *None But the Brave.* Sinatra's legendary impatience was so great that during the filming he threatened to walk off if the director doesn't get going.

" 'When he's ready,' Koch said, 'you better be ready too, baby.' "

"I suppose I was expecting that thin, hollow-cheeked guy in a sailor suit—Gene Kelly's sidekick. I guess I was expecting swarthy or rude—anything but the restrained and pleasant man who got up to greet me.

" 'You must be my producer,' Sinatra said. 'Please sit down. It was nice of you to come all the way over here.' "

Mark Robson, director of *Von Ryan's Express,* had heard similar Frank-the-Tiger stories, but felt he could get along with him. Sinatra's major demand was simply that he be kept busy.

When Saul David, Robson, and Sinatra finally met, Frank said: "Just so I don't have to sit on my ass half the time. Believe me, I'm always going to be ready. And when I'm on the set, I expect to work."

Surely, movies are much like the Army: hurry up and wait. Wait for setting up the lights, wait for the clouds to pass, wait for a retake, wait to reset and shoot from another angle. Wait.

Koch made it clear: "What the man says is what he means. You shoot all of his stuff, then you move on."

David: "You mean you just leave the other people till later?"

"Unless he's in it, you leave it."

"But what if you have to move . . ."

"Listen baby, this story runs up to Italy, right? Well, you just might make all the stuff facing north until you get to the Swiss border— then go back and shoot everything facing south."

"Very funny."

"You think so? He thinks that's what you just agreed to."

"Jesus, we did."

As usual, there were stories of crazy doings on the Sinatra set. And some wild headlines did, in fact, appear when *Von Ryan's Express* was filming in Spain.

Brad Dexter, who had a part in the film, told reporters that he and Frank were having an after-dinner drink at their hotel in Torremolinos when "four photographers came down to the bar with a girl we found out later was an actress from Madrid. The gimmick was obvious: She wanted to get publicity for herself by posing with Frank.

"The director of the hotel was with our party and he made the photographers leave. Meanwhile, the girl had gone to the bar and ordered a drink. She was so mad because her trick had failed that she threw the glass at Frank, covering him with whiskey and cutting his cheek. The director had her evicted."

Dexter said the girl was still in the lobby when the party went upstairs and the hotel director called the police. After making a report, Sinatra said he didn't want to press charges.

The next morning, the lobby was swarming with police and there were jeeps parked outside, with machine guns mounted on them. Two members of the film company were arrested and held for eight hours.

It took the U.S. Consul in Malaga and a call to the American Ambassador in Madrid to straighten it all out.

Frank had to pay 25,000 *pesetas* (about $416) before they were allowed to leave Spain.

While he was shooting portions of *Von Ryan's Express* on the 20th Century-Fox lot in Hollywood, Frank met a twenty-year-old actress by the name of Mia Farrow (the daughter of actress Maureen O'Sullivan and the late director John Farrow). Mia was appearing as Allison Mackenzie in the television serial, "Peyton Place."

The beginning of Frank's romance with Mia Farrow (aged 19), aboard the *Southern Breeze*, anchored near Edgartown, Massachusets. August, 1965.

When Allison Mackenzie was conveniently written into a coma for six weeks, Mia left for an East Coast cruise with Frank on the yacht the *Southern Breeze*. It was a traumatic voyage. Sinatra visited the late John Kennedy's father Joseph in Hyannisport; and there were rumors that Jackie Kennedy boarded the yacht as well, but that story was later withdrawn.

One foggy night during the cruise, the yacht's third mate drowned as he was rowing back from shore.

Frank's romance with Mia flourished on their return to Hollywood, though they denied stories that they were already married. Newspapers followed the relationship carefully; when Mia cropped her hair, it became the fashion, with American women running to their hairdressers trying to recreate that fresh, boyish look.

Frank's engagement to Mia—30 years his junior—was announced in July, 1966. She sported a nine-carat diamond ring.

The marriage—his third, her first—took place on July 19, 1966, in a brief, one-ring ceremony in Las Vegas. A few friends attended, including Jack Entratter, who gave the bride away; film producer William Goetz and his wife, who acted as best man and matron of honor.

Aboard the *Southern Breeze* with Mia Farrow. Frank spent time in Hyannisport, visiting members of the Kennedy family.

The famous Farrow haircut. Mia and Frank pose for photographers following their wedding at the Sands Hotel, Las Vegas, July 19, 1966.

Neither Frank's family nor Mia's were in the wedding party.

The wedding appeared to be a last-minute decision of Sinatra's. After the ceremony he joked: "We decided to be married twenty minutes ago." Then, more seriously, he added, "The plans were made last week."

Sinatra had been in England preparing for a film. When he returned to the States, he stopped off en route in Las Vegas and telephoned Al Freeman, assistant to Jack Entratter.

"Set it up," Freeman was instructed.

But by 1967, there already were reports that the marriage was in trouble. Film conflicts were blamed. Mia was in London shooting *Dandy in Aspic* with Laurence Harvey. There were trans-Atlantic quarrels. Frank was waiting to film *The Detective* in New York, while Mia was working on *Rosemary's Baby.* She was supposed to co-star with Frank in *The Detective.*

Finally, Jacqueline Bisset replaced her in the film and Frank announced their divorce. Mia, then 23, went to Juarez, Mexico and obtained a divorce from Sinatra on August 16, 1968, charging cruelty and incompatability.

A wave from the bride.

Sinatra at 50 was much like Sinatra at 30, still on the go, seemingly indestructible, making more money than ever, and having as much fun.

The year 1965 marked the twenty-fifth anniversary of his career as a recording star. Few would debate that he is the top album seller of all time. He estimated then that his records grossed $100,000,000 and that even albums recorded more than a decade before were netting him $600,000 a year.

"I look upon it as the halfway mark," he said on his fiftieth birthday.

"I expect to swing for fifty more. You only live once and the way I live, once is enough. I stole that from Joe E. Lewis, who is Dean Martin's drinking coach."

More seriously, he said: "As I look back, I consider myself an over-privileged adult who had a lot of help from a lot of wonderful people along the way—especially from the public who still buy albums out there in Beatleland.

"For the future, I'll go pretty much as I have in the past. I may direct more pictures and produce others, but I'll act too. And, of course, I'll play the saloons. There's nothing like that live audience to keep your pipes in tune."

"The Chairman of the Board" in 1968.

December 17, 1965. With daughters Tina, aged 17 (L.) and Nancy, 25 (R.), at Sinatra's 50th birthday party.

Hollywood, July 20, 1965. Sinatra signs his name beside his hand-and footprint in the forecourt of Grauman's Chinese Theater, thus beccoming the 150th celebrity invited to join Hollywood's immortals.

And indeed he did. All that and more.

The day before the premiere of *Von Ryan's Express* Frank became the one hundred and fiftieth movie star to plant his hand and footprint in the forecourt of Grauman's Chinese Theater. As teenagers screamed, a crowd of 3,000—some hanging from trees for a better view—watched him sign his name in concrete.

Daughters Nancy and Tina were there; as were Pierre Salinger, former White House press secretary who was then vice president of National General Corporation, the firm that owns Grauman's Chinese Theater; and Dean Martin, who couldn't resist telling Sinatra: "Get out of there before it hardens, Frank, or they'll use you for a traffic sign."

Frank's block of cement is in a corner of the forecourt which has become known as "Little Italy," since nearby blocks belong to

Sophia Loren, Marcello Mastroianni, and Dean Martin.

Von Ryan's Express earned some good critical reaction, with one writer assessing: "This is Sinatra at his best as an actor, and far removed from his image as a rollicking, elbow-bending song stylist." But his movies hit a downhill trend from then on.

He seemed to "walk through" *Marriage on the Rocks,* with Deborah Kerr and Dean Martin, a film significant only because it got Sinatra barred from Mexico. That country's Ministry of the Interior said Frank would have to stay north of the border because they felt the film was "injurious and denigrating" to Mexico in depicting the country as a land of quickie divorces and shabby officials.

Jack Valenti, president of the Motion Picture Association of America, interceded in

Frank's behalf, but it still took over a year for the Mexicans to lift the ban.

In *Cast a Giant Shadow*, Sinatra had a "guest star" appearance as a New Jersey pilot-of-fortune in Israel; then he hit something close to the bottom with *The Oscar*—according to one critic, "a classic to all that is shoddy and second-rate and cliche-ridden." He fared no better with *Assault on a Queen*, a Clan-type film about robbing the *Queen Mary*. And only a little better with *The Naked Runner*, in which he plays a cold war spy. Frank produced the latter through Sinatra Enterprises Productions. He starred in it as well, which led film critic Pauline Kael to ask: "Why has Sinatra not developed the professional pride in his movies that he takes in his recordings?"

As *Tony Rome*, on location in Florida, 1967.

Tony Rome in action.

A three-picture deal with 20th Century-Fox began with *The Detective*—one of his better efforts during the mid-sixties—followed by *Tony Rome* and its "sequel," *Lady in Cement.*

The private eye role Sinatra played in these two films suited him well, as it recalled some of the old Bogart movies like *The Big Sleep.* Indeed, the attempt to update the Bogart "shamus" was pretty obvious. Jill St. John co-starred with him in *Tony Rome,* and the pulchritudinous Raquel Welch was his partner in *Lady in Cement,* which teamed Sinatra once again with producer Aaron Rosenberg and director Gordon Douglas.

Many felt Sinatra's films hit a new low with his next, *Dirty Dingus Magee,* a witless Western spoof.

He got far better response for a couple of TV specials, "Sammy and His Friends," and an hour with Ella Fitzgerald.

Of the Sammy Davis show, AP critic Cynthia Lowry wrote: "The presence of Frank Sinatra gave the show a special quality. In fact, a more apt title for it might have been 'Waiting for Frankie.' All through the preliminaries—40 minutes of them—Davis promised us Sinatra, much the way Ed Sullivan promises us the big star's appearance if we'll be good and sit through the other acts and commercials."

Of the Ella Fitzgerald special, she said: "The combination of a couple of real pros singing everything from 'The Lady Is a Tramp' to 'Ode to Billy Joe,' resulted in a mighty fine hour of musical entertainment. Sinatra, it appeared, was in high good humor and in excellent voice. He even took on 'Ol' Man River' as a solo."

Indeed, he was in excellent voice. He took three honors in the 1967 Grammy Awards: Record of the Year ("Strangers in the Night"); Album of the Year ("Sinatra: A Man and His Music"); and Top Male Vocalist.

And the gold albums—$1,000,000 worth of albums or tapes sold—were starting to pile up. By 1970, he had garnered the gold for "Come Dance with Me," "This Is Sinatra," "Frank Sinatra Sings for Only the Lonely," "Songs for Swingin' Lovers," "Nice 'n' Easy," "Sinatra's Sinatra," "Sinatra: A Man and His Music," "Strangers in the Night," "September of My Years," "Sinatra in the Sands with Count Basie," "That's Life," "Cycles," "Frank Sinatra's Greatest Hits," and, of course, "My Way."

Sinatra as *The Detective,* 1967.

As a member of the Israeli army in *Cast a Giant Shadow*, 1970.

With Raquel Welch in *Lady in Cement*, 1968.

Dressed as an Indian maiden for a scene in *Dirty Dingus Magee*, 1970. Sinatra is shown here with his co-star, Michele Carey.

Out of disguise and into his $69.75 Dirty Dingus wardrobe.

Rehearsing a solo for "A Man and His Music-Part II."

From NBC's rebroadcast of "A Man and His Music," April 1966.

There was also a gold record for "Somethin' Stupid," with daughter Nancy.

Sinatra sold his two large homes in Beverly Hills and Bel-Air. (One had the infamous note on the gate: "If you haven't been invited, you better have a damn good reason for ringing this bell.") He said the move to his Palm Springs estate was because the Los Angeles smog was endangering his health and career.

The Palm Springs house—16 minutes from work by his $600,000 jet—was set behind high shrubbery walls adjoining the seventeenth hole of the Tamarisk Country Club golf course. (His golf score was in the mid-80s.) It had tennis courts, a salt-water swimming pool, a heliport, and a $100,000 kitchen.

In 1967, he made another big change in his life, ending a 16-year affiliation with the Sands Hotel, to sign with its chief competitor, Caesar's Palace. Published reports at the time indicated that at least part of the reason behind the move was that Sinatra had been denied credit in the casino—and gotten into a brawl with the casino manager, Carl Cohen. Frank did show up for filming *The Detective* at that time with two broken teeth that had obviously been repaired.

Barroom-type brawls, of course, were not unusual in Frank's career. Three years after that Labor Day brouhaha at the Sands, sheriff's deputies in Las Vegas tried to break up another one at Caesar's Palace. Sanford Waterman, an executive at the hotel casino, was arrested, then released, after a dispute with Sinatra, who was appearing there. The district attorney said no charges would be filed however, noting: "You think I'm going to take a case like this before a jury? There was no law enforcement witness, no gun was picked up at the scene, and the alleged victim flatly refuses to make any statement."

At the Trinidad, a Palm Springs hotel, in 1973, another fight involving Sinatra made it to court. In this one, Frank Weinstock, a Salt Lake City businessman, sued Sinatra; Sinatra's best friend, restaurateur Jilly Rizzo; and another of Frank's buddies, Jerome Arvenitas, for $2,500,000. Weinstock claimed he was beaten by Rizzo and Arvenitas on Sinatra's orders.

Rizzo denied it in court, testifying: "I don't protect no one. He don't need any protection. He's a man enough to stand up and defend himself in his own way like any man should." Rizzo said the complaint about Weinstock came from Sinatra's date, Barbara Marx.

A year later, a jury returned a verdict in favor of Sinatra, but awarded Weinstock $101,000, $100,000 in punitive damages and $1,000 in actual damages against Rizzo.

Headlines such as "Sinatra Plus Trio Mix Fists With Newsmen" followed him around the globe throughout his career.

But there were other headlines, too: "Crooner Gives Funds for Shriners," "Sinatra Sponsors New Scholarship," and "Sinatra Music Grants at UCLA Increased."

At the Academy Awards ceremony in 1971, Frank Sinatra received the Jean Hersholt Humanitarian Award, which had been given since 1965 to "an individual in the motion picture industry whose humanitarian efforts have brought credit to the industry." It was named after Danish-born character actor Jean Hersholt, perhaps best known for the Dr. Christian films. Hersholt had been awarded a special Oscar in 1939 for his work with the Motion Picture Relief Fund.

Sinatra receives the Jean Hersholt Humanitarian Award at the Oscar ceremonies in Hollywood, April 15, 1971.

Previous winners of the Humanitarian Award were Gregory Peck, Bob Hope, Martha Raye, and George Jessel.

In fact, it was Gregory Peck who made the presentation to Sinatra, calling him the "current title holder in the soft touch division."

Sinatra, obviously moved by the award, called it "an all-consuming thrill . . . the top moment of my little walk-on life." He added that it was perhaps ironic that "you have to get famous to get an award for helping others. If your name is John Doe and you help your neighbors, what you get for your effort is tired." He held the Oscar aloft and told the television audience, "Mr. and Mrs. John Doe, I want you to reach out and take your share of the Jean Hersholt Humanitarian Award."

A tearful daughter Nancy was in the audience that night.

Sinatra's good deeds were legion; he tried to keep them private, but many individuals in Hollywood, as well as institutions around the world, were well aware of them.

Sinatra had given help and encouragement to actor Bela Lugosi when the famous movie Dracula was committed to a hospital for drug addiction. Actor Lee J. Cobb, during a financial slump in his career, suffered a heart attack in a Southern town where he knew no one. Soon, he was visited by the best medical specialist, flowers came to his room every day, and there was a daily long distance call from Frank Sinatra, who picked up all the medical bills, and then some. "It was the greatest kindness I ever received in my life," Cobb recalled, "from a man I barely knew at the time."

On June 14, 1967, Frank was guest of honor at the First Annual Frank Sinatra Musical Performance Awards Concert at UCLA, at which he presented checks totalling $5,000 to the winners, who received the grants for graduate study in music. A very serious Sinatra told them that night: "Young people believe they can work miracles—and they can. I am here to see if I can help talented young musicians make some miracles on their own. I believe we should try to keep all lines of creativity open.

"I hope we can all strive to bring a little more joy, love, wit, kindness, and talent into the world. If we can do that, then perhaps some of us will stop disbelieving miracles."

Sinatra honored by Israel: Los Angeles, November 1, 1972. French financier and philanthropist, Baron Edmond de Rothschild, presents Frank with the Medallion of Valor of the State of Israel given for "unprecedented humanitarian efforts on behalf of his fellow man." Vice President Spiro Agnew looks on.

Israeli Ambassador, Simcha Dimitz, presents Israel's Cultural Award to Sinatra during a gala celebrating Israel's 29th year as an independent state. (L. to R.): Ambassador Dimitz; Barbara Sinatra; Frank; and Mrs. Dimitz. June 5, 1977.

Los Angeles. June 13, 1979. Sinatra receives the highest honor given to a civilain by the Italian Government, the "Grande Ufficiale dell' Ordine al Merito della Repubblica Italiana" from the Italian Consulate's minister, Amadeo Cerchione. Award is given to individuals whose activities promote closer understanding between the United States and Italy.

October 12, 1979 at New York's Waldorf Astoria Hotel. Sinatra and then-U.S. Attorney General Benjamin Civiletti hold awards they received from the Columbus Citizens Committee, which sponsors the annual New York Columbus Day Parade. Sinatra was Grand Marshal of the parade that year, in addition to receiving the Humanitarian Award. Civiletti received the Leadership Award in Government. At R: The Hon. Mayor of New York, Edward Koch, and Bess Meyerson.

That same week at the Waldorf, Sinatra received the World Mercy Fund's Primum Vivere ("Life First") Award for his humanitarian efforts to aid third world people in West Africa. Here Sinatra hugs comedian Flip Wilson, while the Rev. Bishop Donal Murray of Nigeria looks on.

Sinatra went to Mexico City once and raised $45,000 for the Mexican Rehabilitation Institute. He toured around the world and raised $1,200,000 for handicapped and orphaned children, paying his own, and the band's, expenses.

He did a benefit in Richmond, Indiana, in 1970 and raised $100,000 for the family of Dan Mitrione, a U.S. adviser killed in Uruguay.

When former heavyweight champion Joe Louis was taken ill in 1977, Frank flew him from Las Vegas to a Texas hospital and paid for his heart surgery.

He gave drummer Buddy Rich—his old roommate with the Dorsey band—money to start his own band.

He sent George Raft a blank check when he had income tax troubles.

After his father, Marty Sinatra, retired, Frank bought his parents a home in Fort Lee, New Jersey. When his father suffered a heart attack, Frank sent him to famed heart specialist Dr. Michael DeBakey in Houston.

In January 1969, Martin Anthony Sinatra died at the Methodist Hospital in Fort Lee, at the age of 74. Twelve hearses were needed just for the floral bouquets at the New Jersey funeral, which had an honor guard of police and firemen, and was attended by mourners in 25 limousines.

Frank Sinatra was deeply saddened by his father's death.

He donated more than $800,000 for the Martin Anthony Sinatra Hospital in Palm Springs, dedicated in January, 1971.

In the same year that his father died,

Palm Springs, California. January 15, 1971. Dedication of the Martin Anthony Sinatra Medical Education Center on the grounds of Desert Hospital. The $800,000 facility was sponsored by Frank Sinatra in memory of his late father (in the painting). With the singer (L. to R.): then-Vice President, Spiro Agnew; Nancy Reagan; Frank's mother, Dolly; and then-Governor Ronald Reagan.

Sinatra in 1969.

Sinatra complained of pain in his right hand. It forced him to withdraw from a starring role— that of a tough cop in the Warner Bros. film, *Dead Right,* a role which would have required a great deal of physical activity.

He underwent surgery on his hand in June 1970 for a condition which had been diagnosed as Dupuytren's contracture, a shortening or distortion of muscular tissue in the palm and fingers. The surgery was successful, his doctor said, but the ailment is marked by persistent pain.

Sinatra's health was not mentioned, however, when he made his stunning announcement on March 23, 1971.

He was retiring from show business.

His statement from Palm Springs was straightforward: "I wish to announce, effective immediately, my retirement from the entertainment world and public life.

"For over three decades I have had the great and good fortune to enjoy a rich, rewarding and deeply satisfying career as an entertainer and public figure. It has been a fruitful, busy, uptight, sometimes boisterous, occasionally sad, but always exciting three decades. There has been, at the same time, little room, or opportunity, for reflection, reading, self examination, and that need which every thinking man has for a fallow period, a long pause in which to seek a better understanding of changes occurring in the world.

"This seems a proper time to take that breather and I am fortunate enough to be able to do so.

"I look forward to enjoying more time with my family and dear friends, to writing a bit— perhaps even to teaching."

At the Oscar ceremonies that year, at which he received his Hersholt Humanitarian Award, Sinatra spoke further to newsmen about his retirement plans. He said he would devote a lot of time to helping run the hospital he helped establish in Palm Springs.

"I'm not going to sit down in a rocking chair. That's just not possible. I'm not the type," he said in an understatement.

"I want to take a whole year and just do nothing. I'm going to stay in Palm Springs and maybe try to write a little bit." He talked about the possibility of a book on music.

Would he come back? he was asked.

"No, no, no . . . . After 35 years in show business, I think I've had it."

He made it official with a "final" appearance at the Los Angeles Music Center, in a benefit for the Motion Picture and Television Relief Fund on June 14, 1971.

He was introduced by actress Rosalind Russell, who sounded near tears as she spoke: "This assignment is not a happy one for me. Our friend had made a decision. His decision is not one we particularly like, because we like him. He's worked long and hard for us for 30 years, with his head and his voice and especially his heart.

"But it's time to put back the Kleenex, stifle the sob, for we still have the man.

"We still have the blue eyes, those wonderful blue eyes,

"That smile,

"For one last time we have the man,

"The greatest entertainer in the twentieth century."

Then, a jaunty, smiling Frank Sinatra, his baritone sounding as rich and powerful as ever, sang a farewell to public performing before a huge audience that gave him three standing ovations.

For half-an-hour he sang some of his greatest hits, including: "All or Nothing at All," "Nancy with the Laughing Face," "I've Got You under My Skin," "Ol' Man River," "I'll Never Smile Again," and "Fly Me to the Moon."

And, of course, "My Way," which seemed to have extra meaning that night.

"I've had my fill, my share of losing . . .

"And I may say, not in a shy way. . .

"The record shows I took the blows,

"And did it my way. . . ."

His last song was the tender, haunting "Angel Eyes." Halfway through, he lit a cigarette, and as the smoke wrapped around him he was silhouetted in the spotlight. The spotlight dimmed, then vanished, as he sang the last line,

"Excuse me while I disappear."

Of course, the audience wouldn't let him disappear and, as he had done so many times before—and would do so many times again— he returned for a final ovation and, in the din of applause, he threw kisses and said, "Thank you very much—and goodbye."

Two weeks later, Sinatra was eulogized in the United States Senate, the praise led by Democratic Senator John V. Tunney of California. Sinatra was in the Senate gallery during the tribute, accompanied by Gregory Peck and publisher/author Bennett Cerf.

Tunney praised Sinatra as a master of the performing arts and a man of generosity and compassion, especially in helping children in the United States and abroad.

Minnesota Senator Hubert H. Humphrey lauded Sinatra for speaking up for the rights of minorities, saying, "No man in the entertainment field has done more for human rights."

Middlesex, England. June, 1962. Sinatra wins over a little Jamaican girl—Benita—at the Sunshine Home for Blind Children. That night, he sang before Princess Margaret at the Royal Festival Hall, the first of three concerts for children's charities, part of a world charity tour.

Sinatra in Tokyo on a six-day, three-concert visit for the benefit of underprivileged children. May, 1962.

With handicapped children at the Hospice St.-Jean de Dieu in Paris, a visit the singer made in conjunction with his Lido Cabaret concert for children's charities. June, 1962.

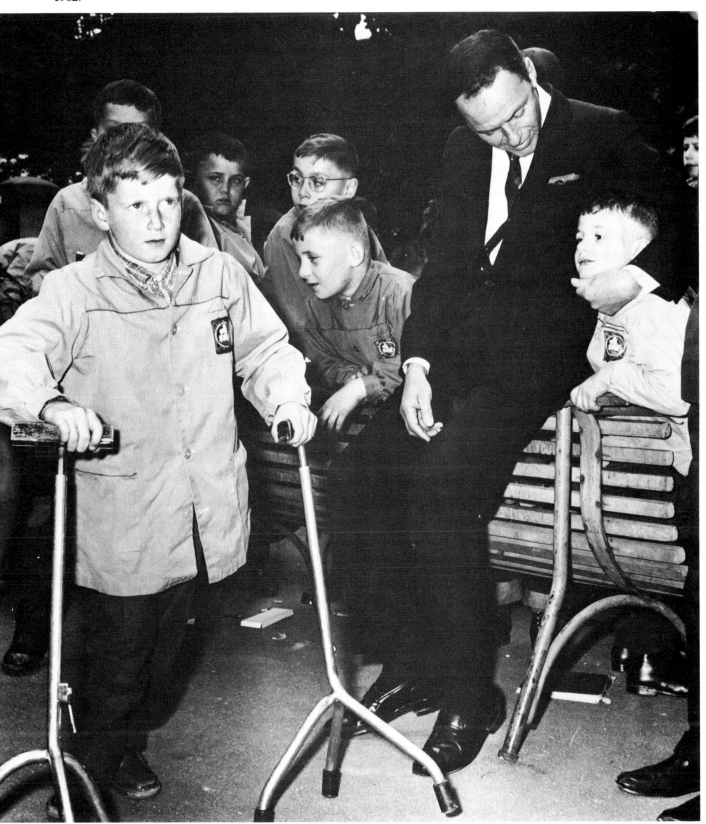

Danny Thomas hands Frank an award for his work with
the St. Jude's Childrens Research Hospital at a benefit
gala in Los Angeles. July 12, 1980. (Thomas established
the Foundation in 1962 to help eliminate catastrophic
childhood diseases.)

"Two legends." Jihan Sadat (wife of Anwar Sadat) invited
Frank to give a benefit concert for the Wafa Amal
rehabilitation center for handicapped children. Here
Sinatra prepares for a performance in front of the Sphinx
in Giza, September 27, 1979.
Later that same night, the "legends" come to life.

Ava and Frank at an Adlai Stevenson rally in Hollywood, October 30, 1962.

Retirement for Frank Sinatra in no way meant withdrawal from public life.

He continued, for one thing, to be active as a political supporter.

He had remained a staunch Democrat through the 1960s, supporting Hubert Humphrey in his efforts following the John Kennedy tragedy. Indeed, when Humphrey developed the flu during his 1968 campaign, Sinatra was among those who visited him in his hotel room, promising to start a fund-raising and voter registration tour for the Minnesota senator who, he said, was "the best equipped man in the country to be President. Later, during a television question-and-answer session, Frank and daughter Nancy were among those who took some of the calls for the Democratic team.

Ironically, Humphrey's Republican opponent—and the eventual winner that year—was Richard Nixon, who was later to befriend the singer when he became a political ally.

Sinatra's switch of party allegiance was probably the result of his growing friendship with Spiro Agnew, which began in 1969 when the then-governor of Maryland attended the Republican Governors Convention in California. On that occasion, Agnew stayed at the home of Bob Hope and played tennis with Sinatra's friend, Barbara Marx. The next time Agnew came to California, he stayed with Sinatra in Palm Springs where Barbara Marx was acting as hostess.

In the next several years, Sinatra and Agnew were to become close friends and allies. The two played golf together often, including a round in Portugal during a global tour by Agnew in 1971. At a fund-raising tribute for the vice president and 2,500 Republicans in 1972, Sinatra made his first public appearance in a year to perform in a two-hour variety show headlined by Bob Hope.

"This is ridiculous," he said as he walked to the microphone as the closing act on the bill. "I haven't worked in a year."

Then, reading from a typewritten sheet, he sang the praises of Spiro Agnew to the tune of "The Lady Is a Tramp," from *Pal Joey*, one of his most popular hits.

"Shyness of speech sure is no quirk of his.

"He likes to tell it like it is.

"That's why the gentleman is a champ."

"He sure gave them the appropriate stamp,

"That's why the gentleman is a champ."

Frank appeared nervous at first; his voice was soft. But as he warmed up, his notes took on the distinctive Sinatra lilt, and by the final chorus he was belting it out.

As an encore, he performed a soft version of "So Beautiful to Know," again refitted with lyrics aimed at the vice president.

He became a full-fleged supporter of Richard Nixon's 1972 campaign, and after the victorious election was invited to sing at a White House party in honor of Italian Prime Minister Guilio Andreotti. This was two months after he had stirred criticism by failing to show

Heading for the golf course with former Vice President
Spiro Agnew, Sinatra's house guest on a Palm Springs
visit. October, 1972.

Republican fund-raising dinner for Richard Nixon's re-
election campaign. Los Angeles, November 10, 1971.
Frnak chats with Nancy Reagan and then-U.S. Attorney
General, John Mitchell.

up as master of ceremonies for an inaugural week concert and, at a party, had had a run-in with columnist Maxine Cheshire of the *Washington Post.*

But, on this occasion in April, 1973, Nixon introduced the singer as a man of humble beginnings, who never learned to read a note of music, but who had become "what the Washington Monument is to Washington—he's the top."

Sinatra sang ten numbers in forty minutes. He confided to the VIP audience in the East Room that as a youngster in Hoboken, "I thought it was a great boot if I could get a long glimpse of my mayor in a parade." Now, he said, entertaining for the president and vice president was "quite a boot to me."

At the end of the show, Nixon said: "Those of us who have had the pleasure of being in this room have heard many great performers. Once in a while there is a moment when there is magic in this room . . . when a great performer is able to capture it and move us all. And Frank Sinatra has done that tonight."

Public records showed that Sinatra's financial contributions to Nixon's re-election campaign amounted to about $50,000.

Years later, after the resignations of both Nixon and Agnew, it was revealed that Sinatra had lent Agnew $200,000 to pay back taxes.

Sinatra's switch of party loyalty began in 1970, when he was named co-chairman of a group to re-elect Ronald Reagan as governor of California. Sinatra said then that he was crossing party lines, at Reagan's request, "to help meet the problems which have been created by the disturbances in our colleges and universities."

That Republican affiliation deepened when Ronald Reagan made his presidential bid. After his election victory, Reagan chose Sinatra as director of entertainment for the president's Inaugural Gala in 1980. He was also among those attending President Reagan's first White House party.

Likewise, Reagan's support of Sinatra helped the singer get back his Nevada gambling casino license: Sinatra had listed the President as a character reference. The hand-written letter in which Reagan defended Sinatra was later sold at auction for $12,500.

January 5, 1971. Sacramento, California. Ronald Reagan's Inaugural Gala at the Municipal Auditorium. (L. to R.): Sinatra; newly elected Governor Reagan; Vicki Carr; Nancy Reagan; Dean Martin; John Wayne; Jack Benny.

February 12, 1981, Sinatra waves to members of the Nevada Gaming Board after they granted him a gaming license. During the hearings in Las Vegas, several prominent people took the stand to praise Sinatra's character.

December 1, 1980 "Ol' Blue Eyes" and the "Pres."

The letter, on Reagan's personal Pacific Palisades, California, stationery, was in response to a note written by J. T. Nevielle of McLean, Virginia, complaining of Reagan's association with the noted singer.

Written while Reagan was campaigning for the presidency, it says in part: "I'm aware of the incidents, highly publicized quarrels with photographers, night club scrapes, etc., and admit it is a lifestyle I neither emulate nor approve. . . . However, I know of no one who has done more in the field of charity than Frank Sinatra.

"A few years ago, a small town in the Midwest had suffered a terrible calamity; he went down there on his own and staged a benefit to raise funds. All expenses were paid out of his pocket. . . .

"Let me finish by saying he would be very upset if he knew I'd told you these things. I hope you'll pardon this hand-written note, but I'm leaving on a campaign trip and have no chance to get into the office."

"Retirement" or no, Frank Sinatra couldn't get out from under the recurring specter of organized crime investigations, which continued to shadow him through the 1970s.

His name had come up during a New Jersey state investigation of the Mafia. The State Investigation Commission (SIC) subpoenaed Sinatra; he challenged the subpoena and refused to show, saying he would not participate in what he called "a three-ring circus." He stayed away from New Jersey, knowing the contempt of court warrant issued for his arrest would be unenforceable outside the state.

Frank's battle with the Commission continued for nine months; at one point, process-servers boarded his yacht, the *Roma*,

Barbara and Frank at the 32nd Republican National Convention in Joe Louis Arena, Detroit, Michigan, July 17, 1980.

May 23, 1976. Sinatra receives Hon. Doctorate of Humane Letters from University of Nevada in Las Vegas.

July, 1977. Sinatra presented Freedom Medal by Philadelphia, Pa., Mayor, Frank Rizzo during Fourth of July ceremonies. Medal is that city's highest honor.

At the Metropolitan Opera House in New York with Beverly Sills and Robert Merrill (R.C.), prior to a benefit performance for the Memorial Sloan-Kettering Cancer Center, October 28, 1979.

November 30, 1980. Rancho Mirage, California. With newly elected President Ronald Reagan at a fund-raiser ($2,500 a plate) for the Eisenhower Medical Center.

Washington, D.C. July 18, 1972. Leaving House Committee Crime Hearing where he answered questions about mob involvement in the Berkshire Downs racetrack.

docked off the New Jersey coast. They found nothing incriminating.

Finally, Sinatra agreed to meet the Commission in a private, secret session. His lawyer claimed he had never been opposed to testifying, he'd only objected to the atmosphere. Following his appearance, Superior Court Judge Frank J. Kingfield dismissed the contempt citations and the warrant. SIC chairman William F. Hyland said Sinatra had "cooperated fully."

Two years later, it was a House investigation in Washington. A House Select Committee on Crime, headed by Florida's Claude Pepper, was looking into mob influence in organized sports. Frank had had an interest in Berkshire Downs, a racetrack in Hancock, Massachusetts, which, at the time of the investigation, was no longer in operation.

It was a drama worthy of the wide screen. And, once again, Sinatra was the main attraction.

First, Sinatra ignored a scheduled appearance before the Committee on June 8, 1972. He flew to London, reportedly to close a movie deal—and to watch a horse race. The Committee issued a subpoena for him, but it was never served. Senator Tunney of California and Vice President Agnew's office later confirmed that they had interceded, in an attempt to have the Committee "invite" Sinatra, instead of ordering his appearance.

The Committee wanted Sinatra to answer questions not only about Berkshire Downs but, according to statements made by others at the hearings, his alleged involvement in the Fountainbleau Hotel in Miami Beach and the Sands in Las Vegas. It was Joseph "The Baron" Barboza, an admitted killer, who had told the Committee that Raymond Patriarca, convicted Cosa Nostra boss in New England, had unspecified sums of money in Berkshire Downs and that Sinatra, in turn, had invested money for Patriarca and Gennaro Angiulo (another noted crime figure) in the two hotels.

According to Sinatra's attorney, Milton A. Rudin: "Because that unsolicited testimony was given extensive coverage in the news media, the Committee has assured Sinatra that he will be given an opportunity to refute that testimony, nothwithstanding the fact that the ownership of the hotels is not within the scope of present hearings."

The Committee recessed until July 18; when it reconvened, Sinatra was the leadoff witness, and it was made clear that he was appearing voluntarily.

But first he made, and won, a procedural point with the Committee when he refused to testify in the presence of the media. The Committee agreed, even though the rule he invoked pertains only to subpoenaed witnesses—and Sinatra was there voluntarily.

He appeared for 90 minutes before a standing-room-only crowd at the hearing. Dressed in tan sports jacket, brown-checked tie, and dark brown slacks, he drew squeals from the female spectators. Sometimes he was barely audible; at others he went on the offensive, telling the investigators he knew nothing about the Cosa Nostra, insisting he had merely made an investment in a racetrack. In fact, he stated, he had withdrawn his $55,000 investment when he learned that, without his permission, he had been elected an officer of the track.

" It was indecent and irresponsible to permit the witness to bandy my name around to better himself," Sinatra told the Committee. "Why didn't the Committee refute it when he said it?

"Why didn't you call in the press and tell them about it? This man's testimony was nothing but character assassination. He was asked a simple question [about Berkshire Downs] and this bum went running off at the mouth. I'm not going to stand for it. I'm not a second-class citizen!"

Sinatra and Rudin explained that they had sent a letter of resignation to the track attorney in 1963 and had received a $55,000 check for the stock. Sinatra said that during the year he owned the stock, he never met any of the principals of the track and, after an initial meeting, never saw Salvatore Rizzo again. Rizzo had approached Sinatra in 1962 about making the investment.

"I never attended a race at Berkshire," Sinatra said.

"Would you believe I've been to a race-track only four times in my life?"

At another point, the audience broke into laughter after an exchange between Sinatra and Joseph Phillips, the Committee counsel. Phillips said he couldn't understand why Sinatra had trouble remembering meetings with Gaetano "Three Finger Brown" Lucchese late boss of a New York Mafia family. Sinatra said he had met Lucchese when he entertained at the 500 Club in Atlantic City, but he couldn't remember the details.

"That was ten or eleven years ago. I must have said 'hello' to maybe half a million people since then. I can't remember all their names.

"I never had any business dealings in any sense or form with Lucchese. I met him once or twice and shook hands. That's the extent of it."

"Would you remember me if I came in, shook your hand and said hello?" Phillips asked.

"If I wanted to, yes."

At the end, Sinatra said he knew about the Cosa Nostra only "from the standpoint of reading about it. I can't say it does exist. I don't know about it."

Patriarca, then serving a sentence for murder conspiracy, told the Committee that he never had any business dealings with Frank Sinatra and "never met the gentleman in my life. The only place I've seen him is on television."

The investigation found that Sinatra had no criminal or illegal connection with organized crime.

In 1974, documents in the files of Robert F. Kennedy were opened to public inspection, and once again the name Frank Sinatra came up. Some papers referred to a civil rights meeting in New York in October 1960 which had attracted many show business celebrities. Sinatra was supposed to appear, but the Kennedys' civil rights adviser, Harris Wofford, recommended to Kennedy aide John Seigenthaler that the presidential candidate not meet Sinatra in public.

An undated Seigenthaler memo said, "It is hoped that Sinatra would realize his own worth and keep his distance from the Senator." But the same memo said Sinatra would help with a voter registration drive in Harlem, where "he is recognized as a hero of the cause of the Negro." Seigenthaler said Sinatra helped calm a 1944 racial disturbance at an Indiana high school.

In 1972, a British Broadcasting Corporation television program hinted that Sinatra had Mafia connections, had, in fact, gotten his role in *From Here to Eternity* because of Mafia influence. The entertainer sued the BBC, and, in 1975, a London court awarded him "substantial" damages.

In 1976, the Senate Intelligence Committee considered calling Sinatra to testify about the possibility of a link between President Kennedy and the Mafia. Sinatra had been named as a "mutual friend" who had introduced President Kennedy to one Judith Campbell Exner, a California woman with ties to Sam Giancana and John Rosselli, a couple of underworld figures, who were apparently involved in a CIA plot against Cuba's Fidel Castro.

But the Committee did not call Sinatra because, according to Chairman Frank Church of Idaho: "The Committee believes it has all of the facts relating to the Mafia and the CIA connection."

When Mrs. Exner proposed a book about her friendship with President Kennedy, she mentioned that Sinatra's sexual tastes "ran into areas which might be termed kinky."

Sinatra's reply: "Hell hath no fury like a hustler with a literary agent."

Still, his name continued to crop up in connection with organized crime. In 1980, a federal grand jury in New York investigated whether Sinatra, or his close associates, had received money skimmed from receipts of the Westchester Premier Theatre in Tarrytown, New York, before it went bankrupt.

The investigation came out of a court brief filed by Assistant U.S. Attorney Akerman, who prosecuted the contempt appeal case of Louis "Louie Dome" Pacella, a restaurateur who lived in Fort Lee, New Jersey. Pacella had pleaded guilty to evading taxes on $50,000 from skimmed receipts he was paid to have Sinatra perform at Westchester in 1977.

The highlight of the trial was a photograph of Sinatra posing backstage at the theater along with its operators and the late crime boss Carlo Gambino, who had allegedly invested $100,000 in the enterprise.

Neither Sinatra, nor his attorney Rudin, nor Jilly Rizzo (all mentioned in the brief), were charged with anything.

Ten defendants were convicted as a result of the investigation, including the late Frank "Funzi" Tieri, who was charged with heading "an organized-crime family."

Sinatra's "retirement" from show business, of course, didn't last long. About two years.

In June of 1973, he told the AP's Bob Thomas that he'd return to show business, "only when I can control the situation. I'm not going to put myself in the position of facing the big, uncontrolled crowds again. Too many times I became the victim in such situations and I'm not going to let that happen again.

"I kept getting mail from people who wanted to hear me sing again. There was something like 30,000 letters, and many of them sympathized with my desire for privacy. But they suggested that there were ways I could perform again without sacrificing my private life.

"I'll record; I can do that before a small group of friends.

"I'll have an audience for the television show, but that can be controlled, too.

"Members of my own organization have been trying to convince me to make a return. My family, too. So I decided I would go back to work—but only when I could control the situation."

In other words, he'd do it his way.

The controlled situation he chose was a television special for NBC—"Ol' Blue Eyes Is Back." It was set for Sunday night, November 18, 1973, and heralded as his "retirement from retirement." Promoters released his new album (same title as the show) to coincide with the program. Gordon Jenkins arranged the ballads and Don Costa the more upbeat numbers.

Appearing on the other two major networks at the same hour were a Dinah Shore special and a movie, *Hospital,* starring George C. Scott. Sinatra came in third in the ratings.

Although viewing audiences didn't tune in

"Ol' Blue Eyes" in 1973.

Frank with mother Dolly, following his opening at Ceasar's
Palace (Las Vegas) in January, 1974. It was Sinatra's first
night club appearance in nearly three years.

in droves, the reviewers were happy to have Sinatra back.

New York Times critic John J. O'Connor: "Well, Ol' Blue Eyes did it. Frank Sinatra took an hour of television and turned it into the best popular-music special of the year. The arrogance, the contempt were gone. This was a mellower and more professionally mature Sinatra. A little older, a little heavier; his neck seems on the verge of disappearing completely . . .

"Sinatra was in control and his instrument was music. The newspaper clippings became irrelevant. . . . The new material seems almost calculated to capture the new mellowness, the effective element of bittersweet maturity . . .

"It's there, and it worked spendidly—for Sinatra, the songs and the audience."

The *New York Daily News'* Kay Gardella wrote: "We thought we were through writing love letters to Frank Sinatra. Here we go again!"

Then, early in 1974, Frank returned to Caesar's Palace and did eight shows during one week in January. He went on a 13-city concert tour, including New York, Providence, Detroit, Philadelphia, Washington, and Chicago; then on to the Far East: Japan and the infamous Australia trip, where he once again took on the press—and the unions as well.

In March of that year, he also played host to the American Film Institute's "Salute to James Cagney" in Hollywood. Then, on April 8, he performed at New York's Carnegie Hall. The concert was a sellout. *Variety* noted: "He did everything right. It was a phenomenon, a ritual, a mob ceremony. They shook, yelled, stomped, clapped together, stood up at least five times."

Mary Campbell of *The Associated Press* wrote: "When Frank Sinatra came out of retirement this time, he proved he's still the "Chairman of the Board".

"Things weren't exactly the same. The audience, which paid $150 a ticket to benefit Variety Clubs International's charities for children, clapped respectfully and gave standing ovations instead of swooning and rushing the stage.

"Sinatra's voice isn't at its one-time peak. But it certainly is good, hitting whatever notes it aims for, with the distinctive phrasing, the telling inflection, the range still extensive, the total professionalism.

"The start was the familiar 'Come Fly with Me,' on with 'I Get a Kick Out of You,' 'Don't Worry about Me,' including those slides to the deep notes. By the fifth song—and Sinatra sang for an hour and ten minutes after warmup acts in the first half—the audience had relaxed and Sinatra had loosened up. Things were going great and, with that security, they went on and got better.

"Sinatra sang 'Bad Bad Leroy Brown' from contemporary music, total master of it, dancing around to a 35-piece band's jumping beat. He hit another of the evening's peaks immediately thereafter, with a medley of 'saloon songs'—'Last Night When We Were Young,' 'Violets for Your Furs'—that was the time to swoon if you were going to—and 'That Rainy Day.'

July, 1974. Wearing the cap of the USS-Midway, Sinatra performs on a make-shift stage at the U.S. naval base in Yokosuka, near Tokyo.

115

April 8, 1974. Sinatra performs before a full house at New York's Carnegie Hall
as a prelude to a nine-city, 12- concert tour, his first in six years.

The following day, Sinatra sings at the Veterans Memorial Coliseum on Long Island (New York).

"Another high point was 'I've Got You under My Skin,' in swing band style, so successful that Sinatra reprised a bit of it. He did a couple of encores, the bittersweet 'There Used to Be a Ballpark' and the restrained belting of 'My Kind of Town, Chicago Is.' He threw a kiss to the first New York audience he'd played to since 1957 and everybody seemed to take it as a personal goodbye.

"Instead of demands for more, usual at a pop concert, there were smiles, applause, and looks of satisfaction."

It was a busy year. After New York, Sinatra did a European tour, with concerts in Monte Carlo, Paris, Vienna, Munich, Frankfurt, Berlin, London, Brussels, and Amsterdam. Then a return to the States for back-to-back performances at Harrah's with John Denver. Then off on tour again.

Sinatra returned to New York for a sell-out concert at the Uris Theater. His co-stars were Count Basie and Ella Fitzgerald (and his date that night was Jackie Kennedy). Then, in November, he opened at the London Palladium—his first appearance there since 1953. On the bill with him this time were Basie and Sarah Vaughan.

By the end of the year, Frank Sinatra's sixtieth year, his office counted, with justifiable pride, 140 performances in 105 days.

Chicago's then-Mayor Richard J. Daley presents Frank with the gold medallion of citizenship at his City Hall offices, November 24, 1975. Daley noted Sinatra's "unsurpassed artistry," as well as the role he'd played in teling the world about "my kind of town."

New York. Madison Square Garden. October 12, 1974.
One of two back-to-back concerts, which were televised
nationally.

Frank accepts a rose from a fan at Madison Square
Garden.

119

Frank relaxes with Ella Fitzgerald and Count Basie prior to their opening at the Uris Theater in New York, October 22, 1975.

November, 1975. Sinatra rehearses for his London Palladium concert, where he will appear with Count Basie and Sarah Vaughan.

September 17, 1975. After his concert at the Uris Theater in New York, Frank escorts Jacqueline Onassis to the "21" Club.

In 1976, Frank Sinatra and Barbara Marx made it official.

On July 7, three months before their scheduled wedding date, they were married at the California desert estate of former U.S. ambassador to Great Britain, Walter Annenberg. Sinatra had previously announced they would marry on October 10th in Beverly Hills, but moved the date up, apparently for reasons of security—and privacy.

The ceremony was attended by the most celebrated of Sinatra's friends: Spiro Agnew and Ronald Reagan, Gregory Peck and Kirk Douglas, heart surgeon Michael DeBakey and former baseball manager Leo Durocher. The best man was Freeman Gosden, known for his role as Amos in the old "Amos 'n Andy" radio shows. Beatrice Korshak, wife of prominent Los Angeles attorney Sidney Korshak, was the matron of honor.

Family members attending included Frank's mother Dolly, daughters Nancy and Tina, and Barbara's son Bob Marx. (Barbara, a former fashion model whose maiden name was Blakely, was the ex-wife of Zeppo—Herbert—Marx of the famous comedy brothers. Marx died in 1979.)

Surely, this fourth marriage of Frank's was the most relaxed. When Barbara was asked if she would take her husband for "richer or poorer," Frank interjected: "Richer, richer."

Still married five years later—and still counting—Frank spoke candidly about Barbara to reporters (a sign of mellowing?) while on a tour in South Africa.

"You know, in this business when you're single, you go along and there's a lot of hoopla all the time. But there are moments when it's too quiet, particularly late at night or early in the mornings. That's when you know there's something lacking in your life.

"So when I married Barbara, I found a better life. She's a wonderful woman. Too bad she's so ugly," he joked about his stunning blonde wife.

"Seriously, she's good for me. She reminds me not to stay up late if we've got a couple of shows to do. Or if we're going to travel a long distance, she sees to it that I get enough rest. Believe me, she takes good care of me. She sees that I eat well." (His weight then was 157 pounds).

"She's really something. I'm truly delighted being married to Barbara."

121

"Mr. Show Business" in 1975.

Frank weds the former Barbara Marx in Rancho Mirage, California, July 12, 1976. Ceremony took place at the home of former Ambassador, Walter Annenberg.

Of the many women in Sinatra's life, however, none was more significant, more influential, or closer to him in many ways than was his mother, Dolly.

It doesn't take a psychiatrist to realize how important a mother is to an only child, especially a son. And particularly a mother with the strong personality of Natalie "Dolly" Sinatra. From the earliest days of Sinatra's career, Dolly was there to help, even though she would have preferred him to be in another business.

And Frank was appreciative, loving; he and Dolly were always close. When he did become a success, he was as generous to his family as he was to his friends. For their anniversary in 1953, Frank bought his parents

a luxurious home in Fort Lee, New Jersey. And in 1970, a year after her husband's death, Frank moved his mother out to Palm Springs, so she could be near him. She loved to go to his, and to Frank Jr.'s, shows and she loved to play the slot machines in Las Vegas.

At 4:55 p.m., on Thursday, January 6, 1977, Dolly Sinatra and three other passengers took off in a private Lear jet, bound for Las Vegas to attend Frank's opening at Caesars Palace. Four minutes later, during a snowstorm, the plane disappeared from radar contact.

Sinatra appeared totally relaxed during his two shows that night and didn't mention his mother. He completed both performances, with no cuts, and joked with people in the audience. Repeated standing ovations kept drawing him back on stage. But he cancelled the rest of his engagement and flew back to Palm Springs to be close to the search efforts.

He decided against a personal inspection tour of the rugged mountain area in a sheriff's helicopter the next day because, he was told, the chopper could not climb above the 7,100-foot level on the southeast slope of Southern California's highest peak, Mount St. Gorgonio.

On Sunday, rescuers reached the crash site after a grueling three-day search and found the crumpled fuselage, as well as the mangled bodies of all four passengers. The accident apparently occurred when the plane, flying at 375 miles an hour, crashed into a sheer cliff at the 9,000-foot level. Both wings and the tail of the plane were sheared off and parts of the bodies were found both in and around the debris.

In addition to Mrs. Sinatra, then 82 years old, the victims included the pilot, Donald J. Weier; co-pilot Jerold Foley; and a friend of Mrs. Sinatra's, Anne Carbone.

Federal Aviation Administration spokesmen said the plane had been off course and did not make a scheduled turn after takeoff, but instead had headed straight for the mountain.

Entertainers Paul Anka, Johnny Carson, and Sammy Davis Jr. filled in for Frank at Caesars Palace when he cancelled the rest of his engagement there, as well as later bookings at Harrah's Club in Stateline, Nevada.

Months later, the National Transportation Safety Board said the crash had been caused by the crew's failure to interpret properly their flight clearance instructions. The Board also criticized an air traffic controller at Palm Springs Airport for failure to detect the craft's deviation from the prescribed route.

Strains of ''Ave Maria'' and ''Hello Dolly'' rang through the St. Louis Catholic Church in Cathedral City, California, for the rosary of Mrs. Natalie Sinatra. Frank was in the front row, his eyes never leaving the casket, which was covered with white lilies and pink roses. Beside him were his wife Barbara, and his children Frank Jr. and Nancy.

At the same time, in nearby Beverly Hills, the famous names of Hollywood gathered at the Church of the Good Shepherd for another rosary, to pay tribute to the woman they knew as ''Mama.'' Danny Thomas, Frank Jr.'s godfather, eulogized the ''matriarch of the Sinatra family . . . a consummate wife,

Sinatra arrives in Cathedral City, California, to attend funeral of his mother Dolly, who was killed when a private plane—which was taking her to her son's Las Vegas opening—crashed in the desert. January 12, 1976.

Sinatra sings the National Anthem to open the Los Angeles Dodgers 1977 baseball season (April 8). Here he's encouraging the crowd to join in.

sweetheart, mother, and grandmother.'' Among the mourners were Frank's first wife, Nancy, daughter Tina, Kirk Douglas, Gregory Peck, the Jimmy Stewarts, Loretta Young, Don Rickles, and Milton Berle.

Ironically, the death of Dolly Sinatra may have been the reason behind Frank's return to films. He hadn't made a feature since the disastrous *Dirty Dingus Magee,* and had been seen on the screen only in the compilation of MGM musical extracts, *That's Entertainment.*

But Philip Rosenberg's novel, *Contract on Cherry Street,* had apparently been a favorite of Dolly's. When the book was adapted for television, Sinatra accepted the role of Detective Frank Hovannes, a police inspector heading an elite unit formed to fight organized

With then-Mayor of New York City Abraham Beame, on the set for Sinatra's 1977 made-for-television movie, *Contract On Cherry Street.*

In his first (and only, to date), television film, Frank plays a New York City police inspector with original ideas on how to crack the mob.

crime. Martin Balsam, Harry Guardino, and Henry Silva co-starred with him in the NBC film—Sinatra's first movie made directly for television.

It aired in November, 1977 to less than enthusiastic reception, although Sinatra personally fared well. "From Mr. Sinatra on down," wrote *New York Times* critic John J. O'Connor, "there are a number of quite good performances wasted in this curious exercise."

The AP's Jay Sharbutt noted: "Sinatra does a good job, but the plot gets mighty murky, the dialogue occasionally is laughable, and this 'Contract' seems padded."

Sinatra made another picture, *The First Deadly Sin,* for Filmways, released in 1980. It was based on Lawrence Sanders' novel about a detective's search for a killer. The movie co-stars Faye Dunaway, David Dukes, George Coe, Brenda Vaccaro, and Martin Gabel.

New York Times critic Janet Maslin thought the novel worked better, although, she allowed, "Mr. Sinatra, returning to the screen after a long hiatus, is tough and credible in his role."

1979: that was a nostalgic year for Sinatra. Exactly 40 years earlier, he'd married Nancy, he'd met Harry James and joined his band, and he'd made his first recording.

So, on his sixty-fourth birthday—which began his fortieth year in show business—Frank's colleagues and friends got together for what was described as a "love-in" at the Caesar's Palace showroom, a tribute from more than 1,200 people to "Ol' Blue Eyes."

The master of ceremonies was William B. Williams, a New York disc jockey, a friend and fan of Sinatra's for many years (along with another New York DJ devotee, Jonathan Schwartz). Williams called the event "a love letter to the man who has given us 40 years of impeccable entertainment." It was indeed a time for nostalgia and reminiscing.

Red Skelton, Lucille Ball, Gene Kelly, and others recalled the early years. Cary Grant was there. So was Rita Hayworth. And Tony Bennett, Milton Berle, Red Buttons, Orson Welles, and Glenn Ford.

Outside of show business, there were former Vice President Spiro Agnew, President Carter's mother, Lillian, and Tommy LaSorda, manager of the Los Angeles Dodgers.

With Faye Dunaway in *The First Deadly Sin,* 1980.

October 24, 1980. With Dinah Shore and New York
Mayor Ed Koch at a private party following the opening of
The First Deadly Sin.

Variety Clubs International Humanitarian Award is presented to Sinatra by Princess Grace and Gregory Peck at the Century Plaza Hotel, Los Angeles, April 24, 1980.

Ceasar's Palace, Las Vegas. December 13, 1979. Lillian Carter pays tribute to Sinatra on the occasion of his 40th year in show business.

Sinatra sat at a raised table in front of the showroom with his wife Barbara, son Frank Jr., and daughters Nancy and Tina.

He entered the room to the strains of "I Did It My Way" and received a standing ovation. He sang four songs during the show: "New York, New York;" "September of My Years;" "The Best Is Yet to Come;" and "I've Got the World on a String." He was given the Variety Clubs International Humanitarian of the Year Award for 1980; and a special Grammy from the National Academy of Recording Arts and Sciences; and the Pied Piper Award from the American Society of Composers, Authors and Publishers (ASCAP). The latter was presented by composer Jule Styne, who had written many of Sinatra's top hits, and who told the singer: "Your music has endeared you to those who write the words and music to the songs you sing."

"You've all been so marvelous to come this far tonight to this shindig of ours," Sinatra told his audience. "I've been marvelously entertained."

Lillian Carter told Sinatra—echoing all those bobbysoxers who had grown up, all those young adults who had romanced to his music, all those middle-aged ladies who remembered—that meeting him was "one of a string of things I wanted to do while I was living."

Orson Welles was, characteristically, the most profound and meaningful as he noted that he and Sinatra had made comebacks after watching their careers begin to slide.

"It's been a long time since Joe first set 'em up for us," Welles said.

Las Vegas. Sinatra receives the "Pied Piper" Award from composer Jule Styne, celebrating the singer's 40 years in show business. (L. to R.): Milton Berle (half hidden), Paul Anka, Glenn Ford, Sinatra, Rich Little, Harry James, Sammy Cahn, Henry Mancini.

October 14, 1979. "Ol' Blue Eyes" sings to a full house in Providence, Rhode Island's Civic Center.

"He is, to quote Shakespeare, 'Every inch a king.'

"Has Frank Sinatra ever walked through a room without owning it?"

So Frank Sinatra began his fifth decade in show business. With only an occasional appearance in films and on television, with retirement no longer even mentioned, he concentrated on what he did best: his singing.

In personal appearances just about everywhere—small towns, big cities, the Northeast, the Midwest—and in the recording studio, the "new" Sinatra sang.

In 1980, he produced his first record in five years, "Trilogy." The album is something of

a musical biography in three parts: "The Past" (also called "Collectibles of the Early Years"); "The Present" ("Some Very Good Years"); and "The Future" ("Reflections on the Future in Three Tenses").

Though the voice may be somewhat darker and tougher, the exquisite nuance and detail is still there, along with the incomparable phrasing which, above all, sets him apart from all other singers.

Music critic Gary Giddens of *The Village Voice* summed up in a lengthy review of the album by noting: " 'Trilogy' embodies all the contradictions and fosters all the frustrations. It's not about the past, present and future, but genius, compromise and hubris."

Sinatra's return to the recording studio recalled an earlier statement of his. The remark underscores his meticulousness in cutting records, compared with his more spontaneous approach to filmmaking: "Somewhere in my subconscious there's the constant alarm that rings, telling me that what we're putting on that tape might be around for a lotta, lotta years. Maybe long after we're dead and gone, somebody'll put a record on and say, 'Jeez, he could've done better than that.' "

And he still packed them in at the concert halls, from Hartford, Connecticut, to Bophuthatswana, South Africa.

He sang to huge ovations for eight nights at the resort of Sun City, Bophuthatswana, a tribal homeland created as an independent nation by South Africa. He collected a reported $1,600,000 for the engagement and replied to critics wary of the political implications of his

Sinatra's 65th birthday party at Rancho Mirage, California, December 13, 1980. Helping him celebrate are Johnny Carson (L.), Mrs. Carson, and Dinah Shore (R.).

Also at the party: (L. to R.): Milton Berle, Burt Lancaster, and "Ol' Blue Eyes."

visit: "I play to all people, any color, any creed—drunk or sober."

In Hartford, at the Civic Center, one reviewer found it difficult to be objective "about an artist who has provided most of us with the soundtracks for our own existence since 1939. But, when the focal point of our observations is in fine vocal form . . . objectivity melts away as quickly as a spring snow and one can simply settle back and enjoy one of the finest vocal artists of this or any era."

Another wrote: "Age may have diminished some of his warm tonal colorations . . . But age cannot wither, nor custom stale his infinite variety as a master entertainer—a singer with a most compelling stage presence, one who uses even the microphone as an instrument in itself, one who choreographs his moves and gestures for the maximum effect, even when it comes to smoking a cigarette with all the dramatic impact of a Humphrey Bogart."

In September, 1981, Sinatra appeared once again at Carnegie Hall in New York. He came on stage without announcement, was handed a yellow rose, then four red roses, then a small mixed bouquet. He put them on the piano next to his glass of red wine, then proceeded to put his audience "on a string."

The AP's Mary Campbell wrote that Sinatra proved he can still mine deeper into the heart of a song than just about anybody around.

"A professional was on stage at Carnegie Hall, old enough to have nailed down how it's done, young enough to do a few strut steps during 'New York, New York' and not look the slightest bit silly."

New York Times pop music critic John Rockwell was more effusive:

"Frank Sinatra has embarked on an 11-performance run at Carnegie Hall and one rather high-falutin' way to describe his work there would be 'great.' Another way, perhaps closer to his own tough-guy view of himself, would be 'classy.' The two adjectives aren't so far apart; indeed, Mr. Sinatra in his own purely American way makes them one. . . .

"If he is the best in the business, he is also an artist. American culture has long seen a split between European artistry and native vitality and craft. Our best popular songwriters have won honor because they can achieve their own levels of distinction within truly American forms.

"But songs need singers. Mr. Sinatra's feisty personality may not be to all tastes. But

April, 1980. Fans line up behind police barricades at New York's Carnegie Hall, to purchase tickets for Sinatra's concert.

On January 24, 1982, Sinatra and Luciano Pavarotti (C) appeared in a benefit concert for the Memorial Sloan-Kettering Cancer Center in New York. The performers received plaques from Laurance S. Rockefeller (L.) in appreciation of their efforts.

he is the master of his field, and his field is the American song."

Instead of a return concert at Carnegie Hall for Thanksgiving 1981, Sinatra was persuaded by producer Paul Keyes to do a television special on NBC. "The Man and His Music," wrote The AP's Yardena Arar, was "a pretty good case of truth in advertising."

There were no frills: no pretty girls, no location shooting, no comedians, no studio audience, no canned applause. And just one guest, Count Basie and his orchestra. What remained was simple and elegant.

Sinatra appeared in black tie, chatted briefly about each of the 14 tunes culled from the albums he'd done over the years—then just sang. With Count Basie he did "The Best Is Yet to Come" and "Pennies from Heaven." With a solo guitar accompaniment, he sang "The Girl from Ipanema." With a 50-piece orchestra, he belted the ever-popular "New York, New York." He offered tunes from his "saloon songs" album, "She Shot Me Down," including his newest single, "Good Thing Going," by Stephen Sondheim.

It was all vintage Sinatra.

A couple of months later, he teamed up with another singing virtuoso from quite a different musical genre. For a benefit concert in New York, Opera superstar Luciano Pavarotti performed his arias, Sinatra his ballads; then they joined in a duet for an unrehearsed rendition of *"O Sole Mio."*

"He is my idol since when I was a kid," said Pavarotti, considered by many the finest singer of his time. "He is king of the stage."

Sinatra did return to Carnegie Hall in September, 1982 for a series of concerts. And while the ticket-buyers no longer wore bobbysox, but long hair, T-shirts, and jeans, the lure still remained: his fans were lined up at the box office before dawn.

Indeed, whether live on stage or taped for television, whether in Carnegie Hall or Kansas City, it is always the King and his court.

A Kansas newspaper headline may have put it most succinctly:

"Sinatra. There Is No In-Between.

"Ol' Blue Eyes' Magic Lingers Across the Miles and the Years."

Sinatra once was asked why, with all his money, with all his success, he continued those concert tours.

"I like to do it," he replied. "I mean, I think if I stopped it would drive me mad. I'm fortunately healthy enough, and I just like to work."

Retire? Really retire? He had tried it before and it didn't work.

But: "If I found that there were certain tones in my voice that were not to my liking, or if I developed a vibrato that kind of wavered, like certain singers, then I would get out. But it wouldn't be a matter of fatigue. It would be a matter of just how I felt in my throat. What condition I was in.

"And I think that obviously would come with age."

One hopes, for reasons as varied and complex as the man himself, that the "condition" will never come, that the record will keep on playing.

Of course, that cannot be; the blue eyes must, someday, fade.

But, the music will live on; that tape will be around for a "lotta, lotta years."

And somewhere . . . New York, New York . . . Chicago . . . maybe foggy London town . . . or Paris in April . . . Sometime . . . night and day . . . in the wee small hours, perhaps . . . or in the blue of the evening . . . Sunday, Monday or always. . . . Yesterday. . . . Someone . . . Nancy with the laughing face? . . . Laura . . . Amy . . . Caroline. . . . Somewhere, sometime, someone is enjoying the music of Frank Sinatra.

Las Vegas Nights. Paramount, 1941. Directed by Ralph Muphy Murphy. Cast: Constance Moore, Bert Wheeler, Phil Regan, Lillian Cornell, Virginia Dale, Hank Ladd, Tommy Dorsey and his orchestra. Sinatra, appearing as the only male soloist with the Dorsey orchestra, sings "I'll Never Smile Again" in a story about the trials of a night club in Las Vegas. (Frank probably never realized how ironic it was; he was just 26 years old when he did this first of his film efforts.)

Ship Ahoy. Metro-Goldwyn-Mayer, 1942. Directed by Edward Buzzell. Cast: Eleanor Powell, Red Skelton, Bert Lahr, Virginia O'Brien, William Post Jr., James Cross, Tommy Dorsey and his orchestra. Sinatra sings "The Last Call for Love" and "Poor You" in this second feature with Dorsey, a musical comedy about a tap dancer enlisted as a spy. Reviewers of this mediocre film made special note of the drummer, Buddy Rich—and the vocalist. *Variety* noted that Sinatra did 90 percent of the singing in the movie and did it well."

Reveille With Beverly. Columbia, 1943. Directed by Charles Barton. Cast: Ann Miller, William Wright, Dick Purcell, Franklin Pangborn, along with the orchestras of Bob Crosby, Freddi Slack, Duke Ellington, Count Basie, as well as the Mills Brothers and the Radio Rogues. In an uncredited three-minute spot, Sinatra sings "Night and Day." His personal reviews were the proverbial raves, coming at the high point of the bobbysox mania. "I'm convinced," wrote one New York reviewer, "there has been nothing like him since goldfish-eating. He even out-manias the chain letter rage and the Rudy Vallee crush of 15 years ago. The adolescent set goes absolutely nuts."

Higher And Higher. RKO Radio Pictures, 1943. Produced and directed by Tim Whelan. Cast: Michele Morgan, Jack Haley, Frank Sinatra, Leon Errol, Victor Borge, Mel Torme, Paul Hartman, Mary Hartman, Dooley Wilson. Sinatra sings "You Belong in a Love Song," "I Couldn't Sleep a Wink Last Night" (nominated for an Academy Award), "A Lovely Way to Spend an Evening," "The Music Stopped," "I Saw You First." (Look at those names: Borge, Torme, and Dooley Wilson—later to gain everlasting fame as piano-playing Sam, tinkling "As Time Goes By" in *Casablanca*.) Based on the Broadway play by Gladys Hurlbut and Joshua Logan, Sinatra plays himself and was described as "more at ease than expected." As one reviewer noted, "Crosby did it, didn't he?"

Step Lively. RKO Radio Pictures, 1945. Directed by Tim Whelan. From the play *Room Service* by John Murray and Allen Boretz. Cast: Frank Sinatra, George Murphy, Adolphe Menjou, Gloria DeHaven, Anne Jeffries, Walter Slezak, Eugene Palette. Sinatra sings "Come Out, Come Out, Wherever You Are," "Where Does Love Begin?," "As Long as There's Music," "Some Other Time." As a playwright-turned-crooner, Sinatra wins success and the girl. By now he had enough marquee value to guarantee movie houses filled with screaming young female fans.

Anchors Aweigh. Metro-Goldwyn-Mayer, 1945. Directed by George Sidney. Cast: Frank Sinatra, Kathryn Grayson, Gene Kelly, Jose Iturbi, Sharon McManus, Dean Stockwell, Pamela Britton. Sinatra sings "We Hate to Leave You," "What Makes the Sunset?," "The Charm of You," "I Fall in Love Too Easily," "Lullaby." Kelly dances. Tom and Jerry, too! A couple of sailors on leave in Hollywood get involved in the life of a young boy; and there's romance as well. Academy Award nominations included Best Picture, Best Cinematography (Robert Planck and Charles Boyle), Best Song ("I Fall in Love Too Easily," by Jule Styne and Sammy Cahn). The musical score, by Georgie Stoll, won an Oscar.

The House I Live In. RKO Radio Pictures, 1945. Directed by Mervyn LeRoy. Original screenplay by Albert Maltz. A ten-minute film on religious, racial, and ethnic tolerance, in which Sinatra sings "If You Are But a Dream" and "The House I Live In." The short won a Special Award from the Academy of Motion Picture Arts and Sciences.

Till The Clouds Roll By. Metro-Goldwyn-Mayer, 1946. Directed by Richard Whorf. Based on the life and music of Jerome Kern. Cast: Robert Walker, June Allyson, Lucille Bremer, Judy Garland, Kathryn Grayson, Van Heflin, Dinah Shore, Lena Horne, Van Johnson, Virginia O'Brien. Sinatra, in a guest appearance wearing a white suit, sings "Ol' Man River."

It Happened In Brooklyn. Metro-Goldwyn-Mayer, 1947. Directed by Richard Whorf. Produced by Jack Cummings. Cast: Frank Sinatra, Kathryn Grayson, Peter Lawford, Jimmy Durante, Gloria Grahame. Sinatra sings "Brooklyn Bridge," "I Believe," "Time after Time," "The Song's Gotta Come from the Heart," "It's the Same Old Dream," "La Ci Darem la Mano," "Black Eyes." Frank's naturalness and easy-going charm are becoming apparent in this film about an ex-GI trying to make it as a singer. One reviewer noted: "All of a sudden it's spring and Frankie is an actor."

The Miracle Of The Bells. RKO Radio Pictures, 1948. Directed by Irving Pichel. Produced by Jesse Lasky and Walter MacEwen. Cast: Fred MacMurray, Alida Valli, Frank Sinatra, Lee J. Cobb. Sinatra sings "Ever Homeward" and plays Father Paul, a priest in a coal mining town. (Critic James Agee: "I hereby declare myself the founding father of the Society for the Prevention of Cruelty to God.")

The Kissing Bandit. Metro-Goldwyn-Mayer, 1948. Directed by Laslo Benedek. Produced by Joe Pasternak. Cast: Frank Sinatra, Kathryn Grayson, J. Carrol Naish, Mildred Natwick. Sinatra sings "What's Wrong with Me?," "If I Steal a Kiss," "Senorita," in a comedy-musical-romance set in old California. Frank plays what's been described as an undernourished bandit. (Frank himself later mocked this one.)

Take Me Out To The Ball Game. Metro-Goldwyn-Mayer, 1949. Produced by Arthur Freed. Directed by Busby Berkeley. Cast: Frank Sinatra, Esther Williams, Gene Kelly, Betty Garrett, Edward Arnold, Jules Munshin, Richard Lowe, Tom Dugan. Sinatra sings "Take Me Out to the Ball Game," "Yes, Indeedy," "O'Brien to Ryan to Goldberg," "The Right Girl for Me," "It's Fate, Baby, It's Fate," "Strictly U.S.A."

On The Town. Metro-Goldwyn-Mayer, 1949. Produced by Arthur Freed. Directed by Gene Kelly and Stanley Donen. Cast: Gene Kelly, Frank Sinatra, Betty Garrett, Ann Miller, Jules Munshin, Vera-Ellen, Florence Bates, Alice Pearce. Sinatra sings "New York, New York," "Come Up to My Place," "You're Awful," "On the Town," "Count on Me." About sailors on leave in New York, adapted from the Broadway musical.

Double Dynamite. RKO Radio Pictures, 1951. Produced by Irving Cummings. Directed by Irving Cummings Jr. Cast: Jane Russell, Groucho Marx, Frank Sinatra, Don McGuire. Sinatra sings "Kisses and Tears," "It's Only Money." Originally called *It's Only Money*, comedy deals with banks, bookies, and embezzlement.

Meet Danny Wilson. Universal-International, 1951. Produced by Leonard Goldstein. Directed by Joseph Pevney. Cast: Frank Sinatra, Shelley Winters, Alex Nicol, Raymond Burr. Sinatra sings "You're a Sweetheart," "Lonesome Man Blues," "She's Funny That Way," "A Good Man Is Hard To Find," "That Old Black Magic," "When You're Smiling," "All of Me," "I've Got a Crush on You," "How Deep Is the Ocean?" Story of a young crooner and those who help him on his rise to fame. Some suggested the plot was close enough to Sinatra's own life for viewers to expect Ava Gardner to put in an appearance.

From Here To Eternity. Columbia, 1953. Produced by Buddy Adler. Directed by Fred Zinneman. Cast: Burt Lancaster, Montgomery Clift, Deborah Kerr, Donna Reed, Frank Sinatra, Philip Ober, Mickey Shaughnessy, Harry Bellaver, Ernest Borgnine, Jack Warden. Sinatra in his classic portrayal of Private Angelo Maggio. Based on James Jones' famous war novel, the film won eight Academy Awards, including Best Supporting Actor for Sinatra, Best Supporting Actress (Donna Reed), Best Picture, Best Direction (Zinneman), Best Screenplay (Daniel Taradash), plus Best Photography (Burnett Guffey), Film Editing, and Sound. There were four other nominations: Lancaster, Kerr, and Clift in leading roles, and George Duning for music scoring. Worth every effort Sinatra made to get the part (originally intended for Eli Wallach), it revived his then flagging career.

Suddenly. Libra/United Artists, 1954. Produced by Robert Bassler. Directed by Lewis Allen. Cast: Frank Sinatra, Sterling Hayden, James Gleason, Nancy Gates, Kim Charney, Willis Bouchey. About a plot to assassinate the President of the United States, with Sinatra as the psychopathic killer. The thriller solidified his new-found reputation as an actor, rather than just a crooner.

Young At Heart. Arwin/Warner Bros., 1955. Produced by Henry Blanke. Directed by Gordon Douglas. Cast: Doris Day, Frank Sinatra, Gig Young, Ethel Barrymore, Dorothy Malone, Alan Hale Jr. Sinatra sings "Young at Heart," "Someone to Watch over Me," "Just One of Those Things," "One for My Baby," "You, My Love." A remake of *Four Daughters,* with Sinatra in the Barney Sloane role previously played by John Garfield.

Not As A Stranger. Stanley Kramer/United Artists, 1955. Produced and directed by Stanley Kramer. Cast: Olivia de Havilland, Robert Mitchum, Frank Sinatra, Gloria Grahame, Broderick Crawford, Charles Bickford, Lon Chaney, Lee Marvin, Jesse White, Whit Bissell, Mae Clarke. The trials and tribulations of young doctors, from Morton Thompson's novel.

The Tender Trap. Metro-Goldwyn-Mayer, 1955. Produced by Lawrence Weingarten. Directed by Charles Walters. Cast: Frank Sinatra, Debbie Reynolds, Celeste Holm, Jarma Lewis, Lola Albright, Howard St. John. Sinatra sings "Love is the Tender Trap," the Jimmy Van Heusen-Sammy Cahn Academy Award nominated song. In this romantic comedy from the play by Max Shulman and Robert Paul Smith, bachelor Sinatra is trapped by Reynolds.

Guys and Dolls. Samuel Goldwyn/Metro-Goldwyn-Mayer, 1955. Produced by Samuel Goldwyn. Directed by Joseph L. Mankiewicz. From the musical by Jo Swerling and Abe Burrows, with music and lyrics by Frank Loesser. Based on the Damon Runyon story, *The Idyl of Miss Sarah Brown.* Cast: Marlon Brando, Jean Simmons, Frank Sinatra, Vivian Blaine, Robert Keith, Stubby Kaye, B. S. Pully, Johnny Silver, Sheldon Leonard. Sinatra sings "The Oldest Established (Permanent Floating Crap Game in New York)," "Guys and Dolls," "Adelaide," "Sue Me." Frank plays gambler Nathan Detroit just about to perfection. The film received Academy Award nominations for photography and musical direction.

As Nathan Detroit in *Guys and Dolls*, 1955.

As Frankie Machine in *The Man with the Golden Arm,*
also 1955.

The Man With The Golden Arm. Carlyle/ United Artists, 1955. Produced and directed by Otto Preminger. From Nelson Algren's novel. Cast: Frank Sinatra, Eleanor Parker, Kim Novak, Arnold Stang, Darren McGavin, Robert Strauss. Sinatra received an Academy Award nomination as Best Actor for his role as Frankie Machine in this daring (for the time) story of drug addiction. (He lost the Oscar that year to Ernest Borgnine for his performance in *Marty*.)

Meet Me In Las Vegas. Metro-Goldwyn-Mayer, 1956. Produced by Joe Pasternak. Directed by Roy Rowland. Cast: Dan Dailey, Cyd Charisse, Jerry Colonna, Agnes Moorhead, Paul Henreid, Lili Darves, Lena Horne, Frankie Laine, Mitsuko Sawamura. Musical in which Sinatra doesn't sing; he makes an uncredited guest appearance in the Sands Hotel scene.

Johnny Concho. Kent/United Artists, 1956. Produced by Frank Sinatra. Directed by Don McGuire. Cast: Frank Sinatra, Keenan Wynn, William Conrad, Phyllis Kirk, Wallace Ford, Howard Petrie, John Qualen, Willis Bouchey. Sinatra as a cowboy in his own production.

High Society. Metro-Goldwyn-Mayer, 1956. Produced by Sol C. Siegel. Directed by Charles Walters. Cast: Bing Crosby, Grace Kelly, Frank Sinatra, Celeste Holm, John Lund, Louis Calhern, Sidney Blackmer, Louis Armstrong. Sinatra sings "Who Wants To Be a Millionaire?," "You're Sensational," "Well, Did You Evah?," "Mind If I Like You?" and a duet with Crosby, "What a Swell Party This Is." A musical version of Philip Barry's play, *Philadelphia Story,* an earlier screen adaptation starred Katharine Hepburn, Cary Grant, and Jimmy Stewart. This time around, reporter Sinatra helps high society playboy Crosby win back ex-wife Kelly.

Around the World In 80 Days. Michael Todd/ United Artists, 1956. Produced by Michael Todd. Directed by Michael Anderson. From the Jules Verne novel. Cast: David Niven, Cantinflas, Shirley MacLaine, Robert Newton, and a host of stars in cameo appearances, including Sinatra as the piano player in a Barbary Coast saloon.

The Pride And The Passion. Stanley Kramer/ United Artists, 1957. Produced and directed by Stanley Kramer. From the novel *The Gun* by C. S. Forester. Cast: Cary Grant, Frank Sinatra, Sophia Loren, Theodore Bikel. Sinatra plays a zealous Spanish guerrilla leader who helps drag a cannon across country for the British.

The Joker Is Wild. A.M.B.L./Paramount, 1957. Produced by Samuel J. Briskin. Directed by Charles Vidor. Cast: Frank Sinatra, Mitzi Gaynor, Jeanne Crain, Eddie Albert, Beverly Garland, Jackie Coogan. Sinatra sings "I Cried for You," "If I Could Be with You," "Chicago," "All the Way." This is the story of entertainer Joe E. Lewis, a property which Sinatra bought when Art Cohn's book was still in galleys. "All the Way," by Jimmy Van Heusen and Sammy Cahn, won the Academy Award for Best Song.

Pal Joey. Essex-George Sidney/Columbia, 1957. Produced by Fred Kohlmar. Directed by George Sidney. Based on the musical by John O'Hara, Richard Rodgers, and Lorenz Hart. Cast: Rita Hayworth, Frank Sinatra, Kim Novak, Barbara Nichols, Bobby Sherwood. Sinatra sings "I Didn't Know What Time It Was," "There's a Small Hotel," "I Could Write a Book," "The Lady Is a Tramp," "What Do I Care for a Dame?" Sinatra plays the lovable heel in this musical comedy first produced on Broadway in 1940, with Gene Kelly in the title role. For the screen version, the hero is a singer instead of a dancer.

Kings Go Forth. Frank Ross-Eton/United Artists, 1958. Produced by Frank Ross. Directed by Delmer Daves. Cast: Frank Sinatra, Tony Curtis, Natalie Wood, Leora Dana, Karl Swenson. Sinatra is Lt. Sam Loggins, with the U.S. 7th Army in southern France.

Some Came Running. Metro-Goldwyn-Mayer, 1958. Produced by Sol C. Siegel. Directed by Vincente Minnelli. Cast: Frank Sinatra, Dean Martin, Shirley MacLaine, Martha Hyer, Arthur Kennedy, Nancy Gates, Betty Lou Keim. From James Jones' novel about a disillusioned writer returning to a small Indiana town after the war. (Shirley MacLaine walked off with all the reviews.)

A Hole In The Head. Sincap/United Artists, 1959. Produced and directed by Frank Capra. Cast: Frank Sinatra, Edward G. Robinson, Eleanor Parker, Carolyn Jones, Thelma Ritter, Keenan Wynn, Eddie Hodges (in his film debut), Joi Lansing, Benny Rubin. Narrator/hotel owner Sinatra is a widower living with his son in Miami Beach. An Academy Award went to Jimmy Van Heusen and Sammy Cahn for the song "High Hopes."

Never So Few. Canterbury/Metro-Goldwyn-Mayer, 1959. Produced by Edmund Grainger. Directed by John Sturges. Cast: Frank Sinatra, Gina Lollabrigida, Peter Lawford, Steve McQueen, Richard Johnson, Paul Henreid, Brian Donlevy, Dean Jones, Charles Bronson, Philip Ahn. Fighting in Burma during World War II. McQueen comes off best here.

Can-Can. Suffolk-Cummings/20th Century-Fox, 1960. Produced by Jack Cummings. Directed by Walter Lang. Based on the musical play by Abe Burrows, with songs by Cole Porter. Cast: Frank Sinatra, Shirley MacLaine, Maurice Chevalier, Louis Jourdan, Juliet Prowse. Sinatra sings "I Love Paris," "C'est Magnifique," "Let's Do It," "It's All Right with Me." Almost as famous (or infamous) as the "naughty" French dance upon which the plot for this movie hinges, was the well-publicized visit of Soviet Premier Nikita Khrushchev to the Fox set while the film was shooting. "Immoral," was what he called it.

Ocean's Eleven. Dorchester/Warner Bros., 1960. Produced and directed by Lewis Milestone. Cast: Frank Sinatra, Dean Martin, Sammy Davis Jr., Peter Lawford, Angie Dickinson, Richard Conte, Cesar Romero, Joey Bishop, Patrice Wymore, Akim Tamiroff, Henry Silva, Ilka Chase, Norman Fell, Shirley MacLaine, Red Skelton, George Raft. The first of the "Clan" pictures, Sinatra plays Danny Ocean, leader of a clique plotting a Las Vegas casino robbery.

Pepe. G. S. Posa Films/Columbia, 1960. Produced and directed by George Sidney. Cast: Cantinflas, Dan Dailey, Shirley Jones, along with numerous guest stars playing themselves. Sinatra turns up in Las Vegas, one of the stops visited by Mexican comic Cantinflas.

The Devil At 4 O'Clock. Columbia, 1961. Produced by Fred Kohlmar. Directed by Mervyn LeRoy. Cast: Spencer Tracy, Frank Sinatra, Kerwin Mathews, Jean-Pierre Aumont, Gregoire Aslan, Barbara Luna, Alexander Scourby, Bernie Hamilton. Sinatra is one of the three convicts who helps out when a volcano erupts on a tropical island.

Sergeants Three. Essex-Claude/United Artists, 1962. Produced by Frank Sinatra. Directed by John Sturges. Cast: Frank Sinatra, Dean Martin, Peter Lawford, Sammy Davis Jr., Joey Bishop, Henry Silva, Ruta Lee, Buddy Lester, Philip Crosby, Dennis Crosby, Lindsay Crosby. Sinatra as Sergeant Mike Merry in a "Clan" Western version of "Gunga Din."

The Road To Hong Kong. Melnor/United Artists, 1962. Produced by Melvin Frank. Directed by Norman Panama. Cast: Bing Crosby, Bob Hope, Joan Collins, Dorothy Lamour, Robert Morley, Peter Sellers. Sinatra and Dean Martin, playing spacemen with toy propellers on their hats, put in an unbilled guest appearance at the end of the film.

The Manchurian Candidate. M. C. Productions/United Artists, 1962. Produced by George S. Axelrod and John Frankenheimer. Directed by John Frankenheimer. Cast: Frank Sinatra, Laurence Harvey, Janet Leigh, Angela Lansbury, Henry Silva, John McGiver, James Gregory, Leslie Parrish. Sinatra plays Bennett Marco in a thriller about a brainwashed Korean War prisoner.

Come Blow Your Horn. Essex-Tandem/Paramount, 1963. Produced by Norman Lear and Bud Yorkin. Directed by Bud Yorkin. Cast: Frank Sinatra, Lee J. Cobb, Molly Picon, Barbara Rush, Jill St. John, Tony Bill, Dan Blocker, Dean Martin. Sinatra, as a playboy, sings the title song. From the Neil Simon Broadway comedy.

The List of Adrian Messenger. Joel Production/Universal, 1963. Produced by Edward Lewis. Directed by John Huston. Cast: George C. Scott, Dana Wynter, Clive Brook, Gladys Cooper, Herbert Marshall. In this gimmicky mystery film, numerous stars play small parts in disguise until they are unmasked during the closing credits; Sinatra is revealed as the gypsy stableman.

Four For Texas. Sam Co./Warner Bros., 1964. Produced and directed by Robert Aldrich. Cast: Frank Sinatra, Dean Martin, Anita Ekberg, Ursula Andress, Charles Bronson, Victor Buono, Richard Jaeckel, Mike Mazurki, the Three Stooges. Western comedy.

Robin And The Seven Hoods. P-C Productions/Warner Bros., 1964. Produced by Frank Sinatra. Directed by Gordon Douglas. Cast: Frank Sinatra, Dean Martin, Sammy Davis Jr., Peter Falk, Barbara Rush, Victor Buono, Phillip Crosby, Hans Conreid, Edward G. Robinson, Bing Crosby. Sinatra sings "My Kind of Town," "Style," "Mr. Booze," "Don't Be a Do-Badder." Gangsters in Chicago instead of Sherwood Forest.

None But The Brave. Artanis/Warner Bros., 1965. Produced and directed by Frank Sinatra. Cast: Frank Sinatra, Clint Walker, Tommy Sands, Brad Dexter, Tony Bill. Sinatra directs his first film, a World War II melodrama set in the Pacific. He also appears in it as an army medic.

Von Ryan's Express. P-R Prod./20th Century-Fox, 1965. Produced by Saul David. Directed by Mark Robson. Cast: Frank Sinatra, Trevor Howard, Raffaella Carra, Brad Dexter, Sergio Fantoni, John Leyton, Edward Mulhare. Sinatra, as Colonel Joe Ryan, leads an escape from a prisoner of war camp in Italy.

Marriage On The Rocks. A-C Productions/ Warner Bros., 1965. Produced by William H. Daniels. Directed by Jack Donohue. Cast: Frank Sinatra, Deborah Kerr, Dean Martin, Cesar Romero, Hermione Baddeley, Tony Bill, John McGiver, Nancy Sinatra. Comedy about a divorce and remarriage.

Cast A Giant Shadow. Mirisch-Llenroc-Batjac/ United Artists, 1966. Produced and directed by Melville Shavelson. Cast: Kirk Douglas, Senta Berger, Angie Dickinson, James Donald, Stathis Giallelis, Luther Adler, Gary Merrill, Topol, Frank Sinatra, Yul Brynner, John Wayne. Sinatra, in a cameo role, as a New Jersey soldier-of-fortune pilot in the newly independent state of Israel.

The Oscar. Greene-Rouse/Embassy, 1966. Produced by Clarence Greene. Directed by Russell Rouse. Cast: Stephen Boyd, Elke Sommer, Milton Berle, Eleanor Parker, Joseph Cotten, Jill St. John, Tony Bennett, Edie Adams, Ernest Borgnine, Ed Begley, Peter Lawford, Merle Oberon, Nancy Sinatra. Sinatra plays himself, and claims an Oscar (in the film, that is).

Assault On A Queen. Sinatra Enterprises-Seven Arts/Paramount, 1966. Produced by William Goetz. Directed by Jack Donohue. Cast: Frank Sinatra, Virna Lisi, Tony Franciosa, Richard Conte, Alf Kjellin, Errol John. An *Ocean's 11*-type film, this time about a plot to hijack the *Queen Mary*.

The Naked Runner. Sinatra Enterprises/Warner Bros., 1967. Produced by Brad Dexter. Directed by Sidney J. Furie. Cast: Frank Sinatra, Peter Vaughan, Derren Nesbitt, Nadia Gray. Defectors and spies.

Tony Rome. Arcola-Millfield/20th Century-Fox, 1967. Produced by Aaron Rosenberg. Directed by Gordon Douglas. Cast: Frank Sinatra, Jill St. John, Richard Conte, Sue Lyon, Gena Rowlands, Simon Oakland. Sinatra as the tough, wise-cracking Miami private eye. Daughter Nancy sings the title song by Lee Hazlewood.

The Detective. Arcola-Millfied/20th Century-Fox, 1968. Produced by Aaron Rosenberg. Directed by Gordon Douglas. Cast: Frank Sinatra, Lee Remick, Jacqueline Bisset, Ralph Meeker, Jack Klugman, Horace McMahon, Lloyd Bochner, William Windom, Tony Musante. Hard-bitten homicide detective in New York investigates homosexual murder.

Lady In Cement. Arcola-Millfield/20th Century-Fox, 1968. Produced by Aaron Rosenberg. Directed by Gordon Douglas. Cast: Frank Sinatra, Raquel Welch, Dan Blocker, Richard Conte, Martin Gabel, Lainie Kazan, Pat Henry. Murder mystery set off the Florida coast, with Sinatra as Tony Rome again.

Dirty Dingus Magee. Metro-Goldwyn-Mayer, 1970. Produced and directed by Burt Kennedy. Cast: Frank Sinatra, George Kennedy, Michele Carey, Anne Jackson, Lois Nettleton, Jack Elam. Sinatra in a Western comedy as an offbeat frontier renegade.

The First Deadly Sin. Filmways, 1980. Directed by Brian Hutton. Produced by George Pappas and Mark Shanker. Cast: Frank Sinatra, Faye Dunaway, David Dukes, George Coe, Brenda Vaccaro, Martin Gabel, Anthony Zerbe, James Whitmore. Sinatra as tough detective Edward Delaney, head of an anti-Mafia crime unit.

The
MUSIC

Frank Sinatra, with Tommy Dorsey, started recording for RCA in 1940
LPs
We Three
The Dorsey-Sinatra Sessions (six LPs)

Sinatra started recording for Columbia in 1943
LPs
Frankie
The Voice
That Old Feeling
Adventures of the Heart
Christmas Dreaming
The Frank Sinatra Story in Music (2 LPs)
Put Your Dreams Away
Love Is a Kick
The Broadway Kick
Come Back to Sorrento
Reflections
Greatest Hits, the Early Years, Vol. 1
Greatest Hits, the Early Years, Vol. 2
The Essential Frank Sinatra, Vol. 1
The Essential Frank Sinatra, Vol. 2

The Essential Frank Sinatra, Vol. 3
Harry James and the Great Vocalists
In Hollywood
Sinatra Rarities, Vol. 1
Sings Evergreens
The Master of Song
The Romantic Sinatra
Songs by Sinatra
Frank Sinatra
Get Happy
I've Got a Crush on You
Christmas with Sinatra
Frankly Sentimental
Songs by Sinatra, Vol. 1
Dedicated to You
Sing and Dance with Frank Sinatra
Young at Heart (with Doris Day)
Romantic Songs from the Early Years
Someone To Watch over Me
Frank Sinatra
Greatest Hits, the Early Years
In the Beginning (2 LPs)
Frank Sinatra Conducts the Alec Wilder Octet

Sinatra started recording for Capitol in 1953

LPs

In the Wee Small Hours
Songs for Swingin' Lovers
High Society (soundtrack)
This Is Sinatra
Close to You
A Swingin' Affair
Where Are You?
A Jolly Christmas from Frank Sinatra
Pal Joey (soundtrack)
Come Fly with Me
This Is Sinatra, Vol. 2
Frank Sinatra Sings for Only the Lonely
Come Dance with Me
Look to Your Heart
No One Cares
Can-Can (soundtrack)
Nice 'n' Easy
Swing Easy
Songs for Young Lovers
Sinatra's Swinging Session!
All the Way
Come Swing with Me!
Point of No Return
Sinatra Sings . . . of Love and Things
Frank Sinatra Sings Rodgers and Hart
Tell Her You Love Her
Forever Frank

Sinatra Like Never Before
The Great Years (3 LPs)
Sinatra Sings the Select Johnny Mercer
The Great Hits of Frank Sinatra
Sinatra Sings the Select Harold Arlen
Sinatra Sings the Select Cole Porter
The Frank Sinatra Deluxe Set (6 LPs)
The Best of Frank Sinatra
The Sinatra Touch (6 LPs)
Close Up (2 LPs)
Cole Porter Song Book
Round 1
What Is This Thing Called Love
The Night We Called It a Day
My One and Only Love
Sentimental Journey
The Nearness of You
Try a Little Tenderness
Nevertheless
Just One of Those Things
This Love of Mine
My Cole Porter
Sinatra the Works (10 LPs)
One More for the Road
Frank Sinatra Conducts Tone Poems of Colour
The Man I Love, vocals by Peggy Lee, conducted by Frank Sinatra
Sleep Warm, vocals by Dean Martin, conducted by Frank Sinatra

Sinatra started recording for Reprise in 1960

LPs

Ring-a-Ding-Ding!
Sinatra Swings . . .
I Remember Tommy (Dorsey)
Sinatra and Strings
Sinatra and Swingin' Brass
Sinatra Sings Great Songs from Great Britain
All Alone
Sinatra–Basie
The Concert Sinatra
Sinatra's Sinatra
Frank Sinatra Sings Days of Wine and Roses
It Might As Well Be Swing
Softly, As I Leave You
September of My Years
My Kind of Broadway
Sinatra: A Man and His Music (2 LPs)
Strangers in the Night
Moonlight Sinatra
Sinatra at the Sands
That's Life
Francis Albert Sinatra and Antonio Carlos Jobim
Frank Sinatra and the World We Knew
Francis A. and Edward K. (with the Duke Ellington Band)
Frank Sinatra's Greatest Hits
The Sinatra Family Wish You a Happy Christmas
Cycles
My Way
A Man Alone

Watertown
Sinatra and Company
Have Yourself a Merry Little Christmas
Sinatra '65
The Voice, Vol. 1
The Voice, Vol. 2
The Voice, Vol. 3
The Voice, Vol. 4
Reprise Musical Repertory Theater Presents *Finian's Rainbow*
Reprise Musical Repertory Theater Presents *Guys and Dolls*
Reprise Musical Repertory Theater Presents *Kiss Me Kate*
Reprise Musical Repertory Theater Presents *South Pacific*
America I Hear You Singing (with Bing Crosby and Fred Waring)
Robin and the Seven Hoods (soundtrack)
Twelve Songs of Christmas (with Bing Crosby and Fred Waring)
Ol' Blue Eyes Is Back
Some Nice Things I've Missed
Sinatra—the Main Event (with the Woody Herman Band)
I Sing the Songs
A Man and His Music, Part 2
Frank Sinatra Songbook, Vol. 1
Frank Sinatra Songbook, Vol. 2
Trilogy: Past, Present, and Future (3 LPs)
She Shot Me Down

RCA: Singles

The Sky Fell Down
Shake Down the Stars
I'll Be Seeing You
The Fable of the Rose
Imagination
Fools Rush In
You're Lonely and I'm Lonely
April Played the Fiddle
Yours Is My Heart Alone
I'll Never Smile Again
The One I Love (with Connie Haines)
Trade Winds
I Could Make You Care
Our Love Affair (with Connie Haines)
Too Romantic
Say It
All This and Heaven Too
The Call of the Canyon
Looking for Yesterday (with Connie Haines)
Tell Me at Midnight
Shadows on the Sand
When You Awake (with Connie Haines)
I'd Know You Anywhere
Do You Know Why?
Anything
Not So Long Ago (with Connie Haines)
Stardust
Oh Look at Me Now
I Tried
Do I Worry? (with Jo Stafford)
It's Always You (with Connie Haines)
You Lucky People You (with Connie Haines)
Everything Happens to Me
Let's Get Away from it All

I'll Never Let a Day Pass By
Love Me As I Am
This Love of Mine
I Guess I'll Have To Dream the Rest
You and I
Blue Skies
Pale Moon
A Sinner Kissed an Angel
The Sunshine of Your Smile (with Jo Stafford)
Violets for Your Furs
I Think of You (with Jo Stafford)
How Do You Do Without Me? (with Jo Stafford)
How About You?
I'll Take Tallulah
Snooty Little Cutie
Somewhere a Voice Is Calling
Just As Though You Were Here
Take Me
Light a Candle in the Chapel
In the Blue of the Evening
Daybreak
Without a Song
It Started All Over Again
It's Always You
Dig Deep Down (with Jo Stafford)
Night and Day
The Lamplighter's Serenade
I'll Be Seeing You (with Jo Stafford)
Whispering

Bluebird: Singles

East of the Sun
Whispering
The Night We Called It a Day
The Song Is You

Columbia: Singles

From the Bottom of My Heart
It's Funny to Everyone But Me
My Buddy
Here Comes the Night
On a Little Street in Singapore
Ciribiribin
Every Day of My Life
All or Nothing at All
Close to You
Sunday, Monday or Always
Oh, What a Beautiful Mornin'
A Lovely Way To Spend an Evening
If You Are But a Dream
Saturday Night
I Begged Her
When Your Lover Has Gone
There's No You
A Friend of Yours
You'll Never Walk Alone
I Fall in Love Too Easily
Stars in Your Eyes
Lily Belle
White Christmas
The Cradle Song
The House I Live In
You Go to My Head
These Foolish Things
Why Shouldn't I?
You Are Too Beautiful
All Through the Day
They Say It's Wonderful
From This Day Forward
How Cute Can You Be?
Somewhere in the Night

The Coffee Song
Silent Night
Among My Souvenirs
This Is the Night
I Got a Gal I Love
I Want To Thank Your Folks
I'm Sorry I Made You Cry
That Old Black Magic
All the Things You Are
She's Funny That Way
The Brooklyn Bridge
Sweet Lorraine
Time after Time
Mam'selle
There But for You Go I
Tea for Two (with Dinah Shore)
I Have But One Heart
Christmas Dreaming
I've Got a Home in That Rock
A Fellow Needs A Girl
The Dum Dot Song
Can't You Just See Yourself?
My Cousin Louella
Someone To Watch over Me
Begin the Beguine
Day by Day
But Beautiful
I'll Make Up for Everything
We Just Couldn't Say Goodbye
I've Got a Crush on You
All of Me
A Fella with an Umbrella
S'posin'
Just for Now
Jingle Bells

O Little Town of Bethlehem
Have Yourself a Merry Little Christmas
Kiss Me Again
A Lovely Moonlight Night
Senorita
A Little Learnin' (with Pearl Bailey)
Once in Love with Amy
Why Can't You Behave?
Comme Ci, Comme Ca
When Is Sometime?
Where Is the One?
Some Enchanted Evening
The Right Girl for Me
Laura
Spring Is Here
One for My Baby
When You Awake
The Hucklebuck
Just One Way To Say I Love You
I Only Have Eyes for You
Don't Cry, Joe
Bye Bye Baby
If I Ever Love Again
Could 'Ja?
Mad about You
Lost in the Stars
Why Remind Me?
The Moon Was Yellow
Strange Music
Where or When
Always
Sunshine Cake (with Paula Kelly)
Chattanoogie Shoe Shine Boy
When the Sun Goes Down
Just an Old Stone House

Poinciana
This Is the Night
My Blue Heaven
Dear Little Boy of Mine
Lover
It's Only a Paper Moon
Should I?
Accidents Will Happen
Nevertheless
Remember Me in Your Dreams
I Am Loved
Come Back to Sorrento
Love Means Love (with Rosemary Clooney)
Faithful
Hello Young Lovers
I Whistle a Happy Tune
I'm a Fool To Want You
I Fall in Love with You Ev'ry Day
Try a Little Tenderness
Deep Night
London by Night
I Could Write a Book
Feet of Clay
Walkin' in the Sunshine
Luna Rossa
Bim Bam Baby
Why Try To Change Me Now?
You Can Take My Word for It, Baby
American Beauty Rose
If I Forget You
Close to You
You'll Never Walk Alone
Ol' Man River
Soliloquy
Nancy

Capitol: Singles

Lean Baby
I've Got the World on a String
Anytime Anywhere
I Love You
Take a Chance
Don't Worry 'bout Me
Three Coins in the Fountain
The Gal That Got Away
It Worries Me
White Christmas
Someone To Watch over Me
Melody of Love
Don't Change Your Mind about Me
Two Hearts Two Kisses
Learnin' the Blues
Not as a Stranger
Fairy Tale
Love and Marriage
The Tender Trap
You'll Get Yours
How Little We Know
You're Sensational
Well Did You Evah? (with Bing Crosby)
Mind if I Make Love to You?
You Forgot All the Words

Your Love for Me
So Long My Love
Something Wonderful Happens in Summer
All the Way
Witchcraft
The Christmas Waltz
Nothing in Common (with Kate Smith) KEELY
Same Old Song and Dance
Mr. Success
No One Ever Tells You
Time after Time
All My Tomorrows
Talk to Me
It's Over, It's Over, It's Over
This Was My Love
You'll Always Be the One I Love
My Blue Heaven
American Beauty Rose
The Moon Was Yellow
Five Minutes More
Hidden Persuasion
Young at Heart
High Hopes
Chicago
One for My Baby
In the Wee Small Hours of the Morning

Reprise: Singles

The Second Time Around
Granada
I'll Be Seeing You
Imagination
East of the Sun
There Are Such Things
Without a Song
Daybreak
Pocketful of Miracles
Stardust
Everybody's Twistin'
Goody Goody
The Look of Love
Me and My Shadow (with Sammy Davis Jr.)
Call Me Irresponsible
Come Blow Your Horn
Love Isn't Just for the Young
The Oldest Established (with Dean Martin)
Have Yourself a Merry Little Christmas
Stay with Me
My Kind of Town
Softly, as I Leave You
Emily
Available
Here's to the Losers
Forget Domani
When Somebody Loves You
Everybody Has the Right To Be Wrong
It Was a Very Good Year
Strangers in the Night
You Make Me Feel So Young
That's Life

Somethin' Stupid (with Nancy Sinatra)
The World We Knew
This Town
How Old Am I?
Cycles
Whatever Happened to Christmas?
Star
My Way
A Man Alone
Goin' Out of My Head
Watertown
What's Now Is Now
Lady Day
Feelin' Kinda Sunday
Something
I'm Not Afraid
Let Me Try Again
You Will Be My Music
Bad Bad Leroy Brown
Satisfy Me One More Time
Anytime
I Believe I'm Gonna Love You
A Baby Just Like You
The Saddest Thing of All
I Sing the Songs
Stargazer
Like a Sad Song
I Love My Wife
Everybody Ought To Be in Love
New York, New York
You and Me, We Had It All
Good Thing Going

The Sinatras arrive at the White House to celebrate
President Reagan's 70th birthday. February 6, 1981.